MW00835025

COL. DANIEL McCOOK, JR.

Dan. McCook's Regiment,

52nd O. V. I.

A History of the Regiment, Its Campaigns
and Battles.

FROM 1862 TO 1865.

BY
REV. NIXON B. STEWART,
SERGT. CO. E, 52nd O. V. I.

PUBLISHED BY THE AUTHOR,
1900.

Reprinted by

BLUE ACORN PRESS
P.O. Box 2684
Huntington, WV 25726

New Material Copyright 1999 Blue Acorn Press

ISBN 1-885033-21-4

Manufactured in the United States

REVIEW PRINT,
ALLIANCE, OHIO,
1900.

To

The Comrades of the 52nd O. V. I.

and

The Sons and Daughters of the Regiment

This Volume is Affectionately

Inscribed.

SERGT. N. B. STEWART, CO. E.

PREFACE.

THOMAS Carlisle makes a picture of "The Execution of The Twenty-Two," in the days of the French Revolution. Arriving at the scaffold they begin singing the Marsellaise—"March on, march on, the avenging sword unsheath." But the headsman's ax was busy and swift, the defiant chorus wore away. As voice after voice was hushed, the chorus was weaker. It wore quite away. It had become a solo. It had become a silence.

The time is coming when there will be none left to sing an army song with a voice made tender by experience.

When a soldier dies, there is a historian lost. With the engrossing cares and duties of a busy life, I have found time at last to tell you what we did and how we did it.

Hoping that I have in some measure succeeded in meeting the wishes of my comrades, and thus freshen their memory in the history of the Regiment and flag we followed, I give you one and all a cordial and fraternal greeting.   NIXON B. STEWART,
                                                    Claysville, O.

CONTENTS.

BREVET LT. COL. J. TAYLOR HOLMES.

CHAPTER I.

A S we pause upon the threshold of this little book, we find that almost thirty-five years have passed since the 52nd Ohio witnessed the terrible death gasp of the dying Confederacy at Raleigh, North Carolina, and with Sherman's army we unfurled the old flag and set our faces homeward.

For years I have been trying to write our story, but the engrossing cares of my ministerial life made it impossible, until one morning at our annual reunion, I awoke to find the old flag we had followed, folded and standing in one corner of the room.

As I gazed upon its tattered folds, a new inspiration thrilled my soul, and we said, "Dear old flag—how I love you." If some hidden oracle within thy folds could only speak of those days of trial and suffering, through which this nation passed, what memories you would awaken—How the brave men who followed you would gather round, and listen—and as they grew old turn their dim eyes toward your faded folds, their withered hands would seem to touch again the trusty sword or gun, and grasping the panorama of the most eventful period of that life, would see it all again; the marching column, the waving banners, the shout of victory. Then will come the end.

And instantly some stray nerve of mine felt down its way at last to that pencil point, and almost before I knew it, I was writing my heart out in admiration and love for the courage and fortitude of those comrades of mine, who were splendid in doing, and grand in suffering.

The Sons and Daughters of the Regiment, recently organized, may find interest in this narrative, for they turn with pride to their father's record, and will annually gaze with pride upon the old flag, borne upon the field of battle by those whose memory they shall commemorate after we are gone.

We turn with fond memory to the boys of sixty-two. We mean the boys, who with smooth faces and laughing eyes inscribed their names upon the rolls that shall, until the republic crumbles into dust, secure an honorable place in our country's history.

Look into their faces now and see if you can detect any resemblance of their former selves? In the gray-haired, care-lined, stern and bearded faces, each march drew a new thread of silver through their hair, each sentry tread beneath inclement skies sent new pains shooting through their frames, each battle drew lines upon their features, each comrade that fell to rise no more, left a sad imprint upon their hearts and memories. The raging battle was never so intense, that a dying comrade could not be given a drink of water, and no march ever so long, nor fatigue so great, that a biscuit could not be divided with a messmate. Such was the sympathy which held the army in common cord. This is easily understood, for behind a war of musketry was a war of mind. Each bullet and each bayonet was guided by a thought and an inspiration whose constancy placed upon each fort and line, or file of soldiers, an emblem of fraternity and liberty, which put to shame the ancient banners of spoil and conquest.

The war was not in all a military conflict; it was a complete revolution in which the many customs, and the whole life of *one* people were changed—and as a result of which new energy thrilled another people.

The war was not all battles, nor all marches, but a struggle of combined intellectual and physical forces. Intelligence and reason pervaded rank and file, while the volunteer soldier never surrendered his individuality—thus securing to our national structure an imperishable foundation.

It will be impossible to give every comrade's experience in the service in this history, yet we hope to give every comrade credit for being a true friend of his "Comrade and the flag."

It was on the 13th day of August, 1862, while teaching in New Aexandria, Jefferson County, Ohio, that we heard the shrill notes of the fife, and the drum beat signals, that Our Country's flag was in danger.

It was noon-tide and calling the children to the front of the building, we mounted the steps, told them the great war had opened in earnest, and said "we must be off." A hasty goodbye was said.

On the morning of the 19th we left Steubenville, O., with Parker A. Elson's Company of one hundred and six men for Camp Dennison, to be equipped and drilled for the fight.

Who can recall the sensations of that journey from home to camp? Many a boy looked out of the car window for the last time, upon his native hills.

They were a jolly set of boys, who boarded that train on their way south.

"This is a good government," said one who had been out in the first call. "We have palace cars now, but coming back they will let us ride in cattle cars." And his prediction came true, for we left Washington city three years afterward in cattle cars, and were four days reaching Columbus.

Another fellow who was chuck full of patriotism said "Boys this is all right, we'll have a picnic, a chance for three things—study, travel and promotion. And we did have a chance for *all* these, and especially for the last, as there were about forty of the company promoted from this world to the next before the war closed.

We arrived at Camp Dennison at sun down, and found for the first time, we had nothing to do but obey our superiors and get ready to whip the rebels.

Our stay in Camp Dennison was short. On the morning of August 22nd, 1862, we were mustered into the U. S. service as the 52nd O. V. I. by A. F. Bond, Captain of 2nd U. S. Infantry with the following list of officers:

Colonel—Daniel McCook.

Lieutenant Colonel—D. D. T. Cowen.

Adjutant—Chas. H. Blackburn.

Surgeon—Joel Morse.

1st Assistant Surgeon—H. M. Duff.

2nd   "   "   —A. J. Rosa.

Quartermaster—Israel Fisler.

Chaplain—A. L. Petty.

Sergeant Major—George L. Zink.

Commissary Sergeant—Isaac Stokes.

Bugler—John Baldwin.

Drum Major—James M. Knisely.

The regiment moved from their barracks at Camp Dennison on the morning of August 25th, boarding a train bound for the front, to share in the fortunes and privations of the army of the West. To pass in four days, from homes of peace and friends we loved, to regions where bayonets sprout as dense as the springing corn, is like being born into a new world.

At Cincinnati we were marched through the principal streets and halted in front of the public buildings, where the loyal women presented us with a beautiful silk flag. Gen. Robert L. McCook, brother of our Colonel, had been taken from an ambulance and murdered near Linnville, Tennessee—almost a year previous Colonel Dan, who had vowed to avenge his death, spoke of his regiment as "McCook's Avengers" and the watchword was inscribed upon our banner.

The flag was presented by a young man, whose name we failed to record. He said, "I present this banner to you, in behalf of the loyal women of this city, as a token of esteem for your gallant Colonel and the brave men who have enlisted to defend it. They are incapable of participating in the rough fortunes of war, but are here today to cheer you with their presence and smiles, and breathe the prayer that our God may protect you in your lives, and give you victory in the cause of the right. This flag which they present to you, is given with the assurance that as long as a drop of blood flows in your veins, it will wave untarnished by infamy, and unstained by dishonor. It is the flag of the free. It has been assailed by tyrants, who have endeavored to strike it from existence. The waves of civil war dash madly around it, and you are to rally to its defense that it may continue to wave over an undivided country. Take it, defend it with your lives, honor it with your loyalty, and when it is returned, may not a single star be wanting."

Col. McCook replied: "I am proud of having been chosen as commander of the 52nd Regiment and permitted this day to receive this beautiful flag—this our country's flag—proud emblem of our nation—this, that has commanded the respect of all nations abroad and all true Americans at home. Soldiers of the 52nd, let us show ourselves worthy defenders of that flag. To the fair donors, the ladies of this city, whose patriotism is always evinced on occasions like this, may you live to see our cause triumphant, and that flag floating on every hill-top in this fair land of ours."

In the afternoon the Regiment crossed the Ohio to Covington, Kentucky, where we stacked arms in a large hall. A bounteous supper had been furnished by the citizens, and was served by the young ladies of that city. We crossed the Ohio river with 981 men, 14 field and staff officers, and 28 line officers, making a total of one thousand and nineteen men. We recrossed the Ohio river at Wheeling, West Virginia, on the morning of June 8th, 1865, with 294 of the same men and twenty recruits—317 in all—and ate our first meal together as a regiment the next morning after arriving at Columbus.

Our journey from Covington to Lexington was made by rail, in the night. The engineer was reported to be a rebel and two guards were placed in the cab with him, and instructed to shoot him if he attempted to wreck the train.

We arrived at Lexington on the morning of the 26th It was the largest inland town in the state with a population of nine thousand. Situated in the heart of the blue grass region, and was the home of Henry Clay, also the home of John Morgan, the notorious rebel raider.

During our sojourn in Lexington, a citizen told me that some two months before our arrival in their city, Gen. Morgan dashed through the picket line from the north, rode up the steps of the long porch in front of the old home, called his mother out, stooped down and kissed her, rode off the porch and dashed through the picket line on the south and was off.

The print of war's fingers could plainly be seen. The fields were ragged and fenceless—a gate standing by some freak between two posts—the top rail of the fence gone up in smoke. Such were the desolations of war.

The afternoon of our arrival in the city, John Allman of Co. E stepped upon a rusty nail, resulting in lock-jaw, from which he died in a few days, and is rightly reported as the first death in the regiment, and from a wound in the line of duty.

It was Sunday by the calendar, Sunday by the sweet Sabbath bells of the north, but what shall we call it here? All was bustle and confusion. Couriers were arriving every hour from the front, and aids were hurrying to and fro with anxious faces. General Nelson with seven thousand men had intercepted Kirby Smith with twenty thousand on his way to Cincinnati. The battle of Richmond, Kentucky had been fought and Nelson was slowly retreating toward Lexington, and we were marched all night toward the Kentucky river, halting at daylight on the bank of the river to keep the enemy from crossing, until late in the afternoon when we "about faced"—foot sore and weary, marching rapidly back to Lexington, through a heavy rain storm.

The regiment was quartered in one of the halls of the city and in the Court House, where we dropped to sleep, too tired to think of supper. Monday morning dawned out of paradise. The sun rose and the mists were folded up, and we arose to find all bustle and in preparation for the evacuation of the city. All heavy baggage, with the tents and stores that could not be taken with us were burned. We drew rations in the forenoon, marched out and stood in line in plain view of the enemies forces, who were cautiously approaching our lines.

Before nightfall we were in full retreat for Louisville, one hundred and twenty-three miles distant.

A number of comrades were left in the city, who were sick and could not be removed when we left. Capt. J. Taylor Holmes of Company G, was among the number. He was very sick and was cared for at a private house by Sergt.

Ross Rex of the same company. Morgan's men came in as we retired, and the captain and his nurse were made prisoners and paroled. The ladies of Richmond, Ohio, where his company had been recruited, presented the captain with a fine sword which he wore. How to conceal the sword and keep the *rebs* from finding it, was the puzzling question with the captain's nurse. However, it was carefully concealed in the chimney flue and escaped the search of the captors. In a few weeks the captain and friend were ready to journey northward and were compelled to walk to Cincinnati. How to get the sword through the rebel picket line was another puzzling question. The sword and scabbard was run down the inside pant-leg, and the brave soldier boy walked stiff-legged through the picket line, after showing his parole. And it now adorns the walls of the colonel's home in Columbus, O.

The 98th Ohio shared with us in covering the retreat. No regiment in the service had a warmer place in our hearts than the 98th. At Perryville, Chickamauga, Peach Tree and Bentonville, they shared with us in the triumph of our arms, and their dear old flag seems next to our own as a priceless boon of our liberties.

That march tried the physical endurance of the raw soldier. Gen. Nelson commanded the retreat with Gen. Terry, an artillery officer, afterwards killed in the battle of Perryville, as chief of staff.

Having no wagon train, we pressed into service for transporting knapsacks, the omnibuses, wagons and carriages of the city to transport the extra baggage, sick men and others who might break down on the march. Sunrise the next morning found us filing off the road into a field near the town of Versailes, which was twenty-two miles from Lexington. Water was very scarce and many a boy was picked up by Morgan's cavalry, when he had wandered from the road in search of a cool drink to wash the dust from his throat.

Twenty-six men were made prisoners from the regiment before we reached Louisville. A well by the roadside was an attraction for the famished soldier. One of these, from which the water had been drawn by the swing-

CAPT. ISAAC STOKES AND SON JOHN S. STOKES, CO. D.

ing pole and "old oaken bucket," was surrounded by a crowd of thirsty blue coats. The pole pointed heavenward in mockery of the soldiers' thirst, for the bucket and chain were gone. Tommy White of the 98th Ohio lost his footing in the struggle and fell, feet foremost, into the well. He found about eighteen inches of water at the bottom, got down upon his knees and like Gideon's three hundred soldiers of Bible story, lapped the water with his tongue, and climbing the rugged wall, went on his way rejoicing.

A matronly woman was sitting on the veranda, directing an officer to a bubbling spring across a ravine through a corn field, a few hundred yards from the road. The officer, taking three comrades with him, cautiously entered the corn field and discovered a squad of rebel cavalry, taking in our boys as fast as the kind hearted woman could send them over. We pushed on through Frankfort, the state capitol. At the breaking out of the war it had a population of thirty-seven hundred and was intensely disloyal. We had two brass fleld pieces which were unlimbered every day on some knoll by the wayside. We were waiting for the enemy to put in their appearance, while not a man who supported that battery knew that there was not a shot or shell in the caisson behind us.

We trudged on day and night, getting only six hours rest in the twenty-four. We felt as we started out on the morning before about twenty years older than when we left home only fourteen days previous. At three o'clock in the morning, of the fifth day we were ordered to fall in, as we were expecting an attack by the enemy's cavalry. We were marched out of camp expecting to make Louisville by noon.

There was much straggling, and the ambulances and vehicles were loaded to their utmost capacity. Two of our company went to a farm house, determined to hire a team with driver to take them to Louisville. They found three of Company C, 98th Ohio there ahead of them, with the team and farmer ready for the trip. The five paid their fare of two dollars apiece and journeyed, without mishap, four miles, when they suddenly came upon the camp of the 98th. The three were compelled to dismount. A mile farther on, the other two were ordered out of the wagon by Gen. Nelson, and they were compelled to march with the rear guard the remaining nine miles.

LT. COL. CHARLES W. CLANCY.

CHAPTER II.

WE arrived in Louisville on the 6th of September. The city was in great excitement Buell and Bragg were running a foot race across the state, Buell was within thirty miles of the city, and Bragg was heading for Cincinnati, where the "squirrel hunters" and "minute men" were waiting for him, but he finally gave it up.

Louisville, at that time, had a population of sixty-eight thousand, a majority of which were loyal to the old flag.

Major General Wm. Nelson was assigned the command of our forces in and around the city, awaiting the arrival of Gen. Buell.

Little Phil Sheridan comes into prominence about this time and is assigned to look after the defenses of the city. Gen. Jeff. C. Davis, who had been on sick leave in Indiana, reported to Nelson for duty, and was assigned to the work of arming the citizens of Louisville

Gen. Nelson was a native of Kentucky. He was a rigid disciplinarian, and volunteer soldiers early in the war heartily disliked the rigid discipline of the regular army, and many of them who followed Gen. Nelson on the retreat from Richmond, Kentucky, to Louisville, and witnessed the harsh treatment of soldiers who sank exhausted by the way, tied to the battery wagons or beaten by the sword, were rather pleased to hear of Nelson's death.

There are many versions of that sad tragedy. We were on duty at the Galt House as corporal of the guard, and have since the war received the statement of Gen. Fry who was an eye witness to the shooting. A day or two after Davis had been assigned to the duty of organizing the citizens, he called at Nelson's headquarters at the Galt House. Nelson inquired, "How are you succeeding?" Davis replied, "I don't know," and he gave similar answers to two or three questions, as to the number of men organized. Nelson was angered, and said, "I have made a mistake in selecting you for this duty," and in an abusive manner ordered him out of his presence. Davis replied, asking for treatment due him as a general officer.

Dr. Irwin Quvin, an army surgeon was passing the door, and Davis called him in to be a witness to the altercation. Nelson ordered Davis to report to Gen. Wright at Cincinnati. Davis said, "you have no authority to order me." Nelson turned to his Adjutant General and said, "Captain, if Gen. Davis does not leave the city by nine o'clock tonight, give instructions to the Provost Marshal to see that he is put across the Ohio." Davis withdrew, and that night reported to Wright.

Buell reached Louisville September 25th, fifteen days after the first altercation, when Wright ordered Davis to return and to report to Buell. He arrived at the Galt House on the morning of September 29th. Your historian was on duty as corporal of the guard, and had placed comrade Joshua Johnson in front of the entrance. Nelson, after breakfast, was standing in the office, when Davis approached him in company with Oliver P. Morton, Governor of Indiana.

Davis demanded an apology for the insult of the previous interview. Nelson ordered him out of his presence. Davis pressed the demand and was cursed in return in the vilest and bitterest language. Davis picked up a blank visiting card and squeezed it into a ball, pitched it into his face, when Nelson slapped Davis in the face and said to

Gov. Morton, "Did you come here, sir, to see me insulted?" "No," replied Morton. Davis asked for a pistol. A friend borrowed one and handed it to him, and walking toward Nelson, he fired, the shot taking effect above the heart. He fell, saying to the proprietor of the hotel, "Send for a clergyman, I wish to be baptized. I have been basely murdered."

I less than an hour Nelson was dead. Gen. Fry arrested Davis. No written charges being preferred against him within one hundred days, he was released by Gen. Wright. The grand jury at Louisville indicted him for manslaughter about four weeks after the death of Nelson, but the indictment was stricken from the docket in 1864.

Mrs. Nelson bought a lot in Green Mount Cemetery, Indianapolis, Indiana, where she buried her husband, erecting a monument to his memory.

Gen Davis retired from the army after the war and died in 1873 in St. Louis, Mo. Mrs. Davis sent her brother to Indianapolis, and bought a lot, adjoining the one in which Gen. Nelson's body lies, in which he was buried, erecting a monument to his memory, without knowing that Gen. Nelson was buried there.

The army was re-organized, Gen. Buell in command, with Gen Thomas, second There were three corps of three divisions each. The first was commanded by Gen. McDowell McCook, the second by Gen. Crittenden and the third by Gen. Gilbert We were in the thirty-sixth brigade, commanded by our Col. Dan McCook, third division commanded by Gen P. H Sheridan and the 3rd corps commanded by Gen. Gilbert. Subsequently the corps numbers were changed to avoid duplication, as there were already corps of those designations in the army of the Potomac.

The thirty-sixth brigade was composed of the 85th, 86th and 125th Illinois and 52nd Ohio regiments. The 22nd

Indiana, Gen. Jeff C. Davis' old regiment, was added to our brigade at Chattanooga. We served as part of Sheridan's Division until we were transferred to Mitchell's Garrison of the city of Nashville, Dec. 10, 1862.

After a march through the city, being reviewed by the officers, on a sultry afternoon in which a number of the regiment were prostrated by the heat, we marched out the Harrodsville pike six miles, and went into camp.

Sunday came, and of course there must be inspection. As Gen. Gilbert passed down the line, he spied our banner presented to the regiment at Cincinnati, carried by Comrade E. D. Patterson, Company C, with "McCook's Avengers," inscribed on its folds, and ordered the color bearer to put it away in the Colonel's headquarter wagon, giving as a reason, that if captured with that banner the rebels would give no quarter and every mother's son of us would be butchered. Some time afterward the flag was brought out, and carried through all our marches and battles. When the end came, its texture had been whipped and worn out by the winds and waves on the bloody fields of the south land.

When the last review at Washington was over, a piece about as broad as your two hands, was all that was left of it. The boys hunted up the new state flag—with the words "E Pluribus unum" on it, which had followed us from Cincinnati, stowed away in a baggage wagon, and nailed it on the old staff, and it now stands in the flag room of the Capitol. Its folds are more tender than tissue paper, and in another forty years, it will be little more than dust and ashes.

The first night in camp at the six mile house, we were directed to put everything in readiness for rapid movements, as we were elected to drive Bragg, who was at or near Bardstown, out of Kentucky.

Alfred Robinson, of Company B, was severely injured just after going into camp. Exhausted by the march, he

¹ay down beside a log, and covering himself with leaves, fell into a sound sleep. When uncle Tom, the colored cook of Company K, returning from the creek below with two buckets of water, crossed over the log, planting both feet on Robinson's breast He was sent to the hospital and was discharged from the service on account of the injury.

J. C. HARRISON, CO. B.

Four hours, drill, the few days we stayed here, gave us an appetite for army rations. One thing we were grateful for, was good coffee and plenty of it. Some one in Congress proposed the substitution of tea for coffee and declared the soldiers would welcome the change. Not so, coffee was the "true water of life," his solace and his main-stay. When a boy could not drink his coffee, he might as well be sent to the rear. A soldier could make his coffee in five minutes, drink it in three, grind a hard tack and feel as refreshed as though he had finished a fifty-cent dinner.

We started on the hunt of Bragg's army Oct. 2nd, only six weeks since we left home, yet we marched away that morning with a swinging step, like old veterans. But, before nightfall came, many a poor fellow lay by the roadside nursing his blistered feet.

I think the army never felt such a sense of loneliness, as when we passed through Kentucky in that campaign. The name signifies "The dark and bloody ground." The villages seemed to be asleep like a lazy dog in the hot sunshine. Stores closed, shops deserted and the roads dotted with the *inkiest* heads imaginable, as if some Ethiopian had suddenly taken possession of the land.

What a difference there was between fleeing from a foe and pursuing one. Sleep unbroken, wearied and foot-sore, the soldier lay down with his head on Jacob's pillow. It may have been a Bethel to him, where wife or child or "the girl he left behind him" may be ascending or descending in the guise of angels on the silver ladder of a dream.

On the third day's march, one of our boys was taken sick and we were left to care for him until the ambulance came up. After getting him in the ambulance we started to overtake the regiment, a task which took the the remainder of the day and far into the night, encountering much the same difficulties met by "Si Kleg" except in the outcome.

On the evening of the 7th we went into camp about eleven o'clock, having made a little over fifteen miles per day. Everywhere Bragg had posted frantic proclamations to the people of Kentucky to rise in their might and expel the invaders from their sacred soil. Gilbert's corps was heading for Perryville by the Springfield pike. McCook's by the Mackville pike and Crittenden's by the Broomfield pike.

Sheridan's Division was in the advance. Mitchell's and Shoeff's on our left.

We crossed Doctor's Creek at three o'clock on the next morning, the 52nd in the advance, Company A on the skirmish line. The moon was shining clear, when our line moved up to the summit, driving the enemy's pickets in to their reserve, without the loss of a man. Barnett's 2nd Illinois

CAPT. F. B. JAMES, CO. I.

Battery was brought up and planted on the brow of the hill. The 52nd formed in the rear of the Battery, the 85th to our right, the 125th to our right and rear, and the 86th in the reserve. At 10 a. m. we were moved out in front, down through the woods, supporting the 44th Illinois and 2nd Missouri of Carlin's Brigade. While in this position we were within a short distance of the burnt barn and cornfield where Jackson and Terry fell in the afternoon. The enemy charged our line twice between 10 and 12 o'clock, but were repulsed with heavy loss by the regiments in front of us, the 2nd Missouri losing heavily in the first charge.

We were moved back to the ridge at noon, taking position between Hancock's and Barnett's Batteries, where we lay all the afternoon. At four o'clock the enemy massed in our front. The charge was led by Gen. Kline, who was riding a white horse. A shell from our Battery struck the horse, killing the rider. The line was broken and they retreated in confusion.

The brunt of the battle fell upon McCook's corps. Our position gave us a fine view of the battle in the afternoon, especially on our left, where the field was more hotly contested. Charge after charge was made on Terry's division and the odds were against us, but our men would rally and the tide would turn in our favor. A brigade of reinforcements brought a cheer all along our lines and fresh courage to our brave men. A rebel shell exploded in a caisson, and horses and men were lifted in the air. The gallant 98th had their first baptism of blood, losing heavily in men and officers, among the number was Col. Webster, a noble man and a hero, also their Division Commander, Gen. Jackson.

Our loss in the regiment was light. The first man struck in the battle was George Wilson of Company E,— shot through the hand, early in the morning. There were two deaths from wounds, while our total loss was fourteen. Gen. Buell has been severely and no doubt justly criticized for the result of that battle. Col. Hinman of the Sherman Brigade says in his history. "We saw two or three divisions lying idly on their arms taking no part whatever in the conflict. In truth this is what we did a mile from the battlefield. Our division filed off into the woods, formed in line, and lay down. This was our part of the battle of Perryville. We lay all the afternoon, almost in view of the battle, wondering why we did not participate.''

Gen. Gilbert wrote to Gen. Carlin in eighty-five, "that he left the front at eleven o'clock and until nearly 4 p. m. had no knowledge that there was any fighting going on in

SERGT. H. B. TREAT, CO. I.

front of Sheridan's division until the final attack by Gen. Kline at 3:45 p. m. in front of the two batteries and our brigade with two regiments of Carlin's that supported them.''

The facts are that the battle was fought by McCook's corps and by two of his three divisions with a part of Sheridan's division against three divisions of the enemy under Gen. Polk and a division of Hardee's corps. Our loss was over four thousand while twenty-three thousand of our men were not engaged. Gen. Chas. C. Gilbert is lost sight of from this time. He continued with the army until June '63, commanding a division, when Col. Opdycke of the 125th Ohio, wrote to Senator Wade of Ohio, informing him, "that Gilbert had attempted to have a young man commissioned as an officer in his regiment. Believing that no civilian should gain a place that ought to be reserved as a reward for meritorious conduct of our own men in the ranks, he objected and reminded the senator that Gilbert was a captain in the regular army and had been appointed and was acting as brigadier general and his appointment had not been confirmed by the senate." In a short time the senate failed to confirm and Capt. Gilbert was ordered to duty elsewhere. Thus his military career was wrecked. Carlin's Brigade was within half a mile of Perryville by sundown and Bragg was in retreat before morning.

We passed over the battlefield the next morning. Bodies of men and horses lay scattered about everywhere, every house and barn was filled with the maimed, the dying and dead. The battle is the red blossom of war, but the roots dark and bitter run beneath the tents, creep through the wards of the hospitals and feel their way, like the fingers of the hand, in all this ground we tread upon—save that only where lie our dead.

If any one thinks that when our men are stricken upon the field of battle they fill the air with cries and groans, he greatly errs. An arm is shattered, a leg carried away, a bullet pierces the breast, and the soldier sinks down silently upon the ground or creeps away, if he can, without a mur-

mur or complaint, falls as the sparrow falls, speechless—
and I earnestly believe, not without the Father's notice.

The dying horse gives out his fearful utterance of almost human suffering, but the mangled rider is dumb. The
crash of musketry, the roar of artillery; the shriek of shells,
the rebel yell, the yankee cheer, make up the voices of the
battle field. In company with a comrade we started in
search of the 98th to find out how the regiment had fared,
as it had been in the hottest of the fight the day before. The
regiment was burying their dead, our comrade asked for his
brother,—"there he lies," said one of his comrades, "brave
boy he was, he fell with his face to the foe."

Passing a building where the enemy had left their
wounded, we were attracted by the cry of a rebel drummer
boy. He was in the delirium of death. Some one had
leaned a broad plank against the side of the building where
he lay, to keep the drip from the eaves of the house from
falling in his face, for it was raining as it always did after a
battle. I shall never forget that sweet, childish voice; he
said in his delirium; "mother, dear mother, why don't you
come and take me home?" That mother did not come. She
lived far away, perhaps in some beautiful home in the sunny
south. She never saw her boy again, for as we returned,
his form was still, his childish voice was hushed in death
and we thought may it not be that the angels did come and
take him to the home above.

JOHN J. McCOOK.

CHAPTER III.

PERRYVILLE was a small town of three or four hundred, situated on Chaplain river, ten miles west of Danville, forty-five miles south of Lexington, and eighty-five from Louisville. Bragg was in full retreat for Cumberland gap. He had stripped the country of every thing to eat, drink or to wear.

We marched toward Crab Orchard, camping on the north fork of Salt river. Every stream seemed to be a river in the south. This branch was small and almost dry.

Buell issued strict orders not to touch anything belonging to friend or foe. This was not without reason, for Kentucky was a loyal state. She furnished sixty thousand soldiers for the Union army. In spite of all this, a desire for more than army rations was continually cropping out. While resting on Salt river, a member of Company F returning from picket, found a bee hive that had been carried out from a farm house by rebel cavalry. They had left some honey in the box. Our comrade who brought away the remainder, was arrested. A drum head court martial was called and he was marched through the camp with a board strapped to his knapsack on which was written the word "thief." He was dismissed from the service in disgrace Oct. 16th, 1862. Gen. Cruft, Buell's chief of staff, called the court martial and executed the sentence. In less than three months the comrade re-enlisted in the 126th Ohio and was at the surrender of Lee at Appomattox.

Our movement toward Nashville began about the 18th of October and brought us within three or four miles of the famous Mammoth Cave. In company with other members of the regiment, under the direction of Adjutant Chas. H. Blackburn, we spent a day exploring its wonders, returning in the evening, glad we had visited nature's wonderful cavern. Our halt at Cave City was followed by several days hard marching. It rained and turned to snow. Our cloth-

W. J. FUNSTON, CO. E.

ing froze and became stiff as boards. The suffering of such a march is beyond the power of words to portray. We trudged along as best we could, making about 15 miles a day. At Pruits Knob, Co. F lost its first man by death. It was Cornelius Hess, who died of measles, and was buried with the honors of war. On the march, while resting by the roadside, two men, one of Company E, another from Company D, accidentally or otherwise, shot off the index finger of the right hand. Col. McCook declared with emphasis that they should not be discharged while the war lasted, and they should be made to carry wood and water for the regiment.

We arrived at Edgefield, across the Cumberland from Nashville, about the first of November, where we went into camp for awhile. It was here we had our first experience at a soldiers' corn husking. One morning we started up the Cumberland with about four hundred men and thirty teams. A regiment of cavalry had taken the advance to clear the way. Twelve miles from camp we found a field of splendid corn, with kernels as clean and white and firm as the teeth Richard was born with. Twenty-five men went along the rows, mounted on mules, and with sharp sabers, severed the ears from the stalks, husk and all. We followed after with wagons, gathering up the corn, going through the field like a tornado. In a little over an hour, we filled the wagons and back we went to the camp. No children's happy shouts follow the reapers. No mother's smile welcomes them home. This is one of the stern realities of war, from which we were released when peace came.

It was here that we had our first introduction to that essential of army appendages, the sutler. Many people did not care whether the war closed or not. They were destined to get rich. Money sharks followed the army, while trade bustled along on the heels of war. Did you ever see a sutler's tent? The bait hung out—sometimes one thing— sometimes another. Plenty of knick-knacks and nothings that sold at starvation prices. Water suspected of having a lemon dipped in it—a dime for two swallows. Pencils whose lead—unlike that of the rebel bullet, does not go quite through, are good for a quarter, as the apothecary says, "and so on." Prices that took away your breath as well as your cash.

Checks were issued to the boys when they were found strapped, and the sutler always came up with a broad grin, when the man with the iron box came round. Our sutler was a profane fellow, who was lacking in the genial element

LIEUT. W. P. MILVANE, CO. D.

of social life. One night at Brentwood the boys cut the stays of his tent, confiscated his goods and whooped him out of camp, and Mr. Baldwin dropped out of sight with the 52nd.

November 4th we passed through Nashville to Mill Creek, six miles south-east of the city on the Nolensville pike, where we pitched our tents in the soldier's paradise, known as Camp Sheridan. We were here five weeks, during which time the measles infected the camp and many died in the hospital with them, also many had fatal pneumonia.

We drilled six hours a day, when not on other duty. Quite a number of old regiments were in the division, among the number the 8th Wisconsin, composed mostly of "lumbermen," and they were the cleanliest set of men in the service. In the 14th Michigan were two companies of half-breed Indians, who were famous for their drill as skirmishers.

A foot race was arranged between the 8th Wisconsin, 14th Michigan, 85th Illinois and 52nd Ohio, the prize being a silk guidon or marker. It was placed on a hill, half a mile away. The soldier who touched the flag first, was to bear it away as the prize of his regiment. The race was very exciting. Down into the valley and up the slopes we went, yelling at every step. Little Phil leading the charge with his hat on the point of his sword, riding the same horse that was shot from under him at Stone River six weeks later. The flag was reached by Billy Armstrong of Company H, of our regiment, and he was placed upon the shoulders of his comrades and borne into camp in triumph.

Camp life was not conducive to contentment in our army experience. We were busy drilling and policing our camp, but thoughts of home and friends grew more intense. Letters came. They spoke of Thanksgiving. There was to be song and sermon in the old church. The table spread and all the children home but the loyal soldier boys. And the loyal land would send up a song and psalm for the blessings it had numbered. Some grew homesick and died of the terrible longing for home. The symptoms were, languor, debility, low fever, loss of appetite—*death*. But he who died thus, gave his life as truly as if a bullet had found his heart. Loved ones at home had something to answer for. Many a boy died, just because his dearest friends did not send him a prescription twice a week—price three cents.

But it was not all dull and dreary in camp. The only thing was, that it was so unlike home. Not a familiar sound in it all. No sweet Sabbath bells, no lowing herds, no chanticleer's shrill crow, no rattling pavements, no shutting

G. L. PATTERSON, CO. D.

doors—what was there to cheer the heart and revive the spirits? Hark! At break of day from field and wood and hill, come the sweet notes of the reveille. Bugle answers to bugle, fifes warble, and through the roaring of the drum you catch the soul stirring swell of a full band, playing in an unseen camp. There is music everywhere. When the martial strains have ceased, the contrast begins in the hideous braying of the immense camp of mules. How the konk-konk-konkle of the sub-basso rises and swells and echoes in solemn discord. The mule in the army was an institution dead or alive. How he was abused. No wonder he brayed in his rusty way. He is the only creature that can slip all his misery to the end of his tongue. Mark Twain says, "It's tail is a miserable wisp, its mane is a worn out shoe-brush, its ears the chief end of it, and yet ugly as it is, no steed ever had so beautiful a foot."

There is something soul-inspiring at early dawn when everything is astir in camp. Flags begin to float in the breeze. Blue threads of smoke curl up along the camps—soon you hear the click of the butt end of a bayonet, beating coffee in a tin cup, giving you the merry music of the soldier's coffee mill. And then, you are bugled to breakfast, bugled to guard mounting, bugled to dinner, bugled to battle and bugled to bed. A soldier could sleep anywhere, except on duty. We have slept on a couple of rails, laid side by side, muttering thanks to the man who invented sleep, as Sancho Panzo did.

December 10th we moved into the city of Nashville, being transferred from Sheridan's Division to Gen. Mitchell's, then on garrison duty in the city. Our camp was on the Franklin pike. The memories of our stay there would fill this little book. There was grand old Fort Negley, with its parapets and black-mouthed siege guns. The sentries upon the walls could be seen at all hours of the day, and the watchman as upon Mt. Seir in answer to the challenge, "What of the night?" shouted—"twelve o'clock, and all is well!"

And just to think in that cave on the hillside, fifty feet or more from the entrance, was found a sparkling spring of pure water, strong enough for an army. No cesspool of filth from the city to pollute it, as it came from the south of our camp.

And the Sibley tent with its immortal tripod in the center, on which hung the fire-pot that made us look like "smoked yankees." How we have been haunted by these pictures of memory, as we have gone back in our dreams since the war, and drank of that spring, languished in the guard house for some slight neglect, or milked the cows on the common, or watched out the night by the cot on which

N. H. BOSTWICK, CO. I.

rested the fevered form of a comrade we loved. Nashville had about 18,000 population then. It has 90,000 now. Then it was a tented town. Her streets pulsated all day long like a heart with one incessant, turbulent stream of living beings. There were Africans, ambulances, ammunition, brigades, batteries, beasts, bread, bacon, men, mules and so on to the end of the alphabet, all crowded together in one promiscuous throng. Our duty consisted in picketing, unloading boats, guarding trains to the front, and patrolling the city. Had we been given our choice we would have taken our chances at the front. There was very little time for drill. A detail from the regiment, of sixty men, three times a week went by rail as train guard to the front.

Accidents occurred almost every week. Three of the regiment were killed and fifteen wounded by trains being derailed or wrecked by torpedoes placed under the ties. Trains were fired upon by the bushwhackers concealed by the roadside. Unlike soldiering at the front, we were here, there and everywhere—today on picket, tomorrow on detail, all without regularity; and it told upon the endurance of the men

But the days flow by in an unbroken stream A month passes and you fancy it is not half gone. When you stopped to think, you find you have lost your reckonings. Occasionally you meet a boy who is hunting up the day of the week. The Sabbath, that sweet blossom in the waste of time, is trampled by hurrying feet, unnoticed. It came and went yesterday, and you find it out tomorrow. You seem to be absorbed like the man of the world. Yet when the Sabbaths began to drop out of your calendar in the army, you felt somewhat uncomfortable for a sinner— and a feeling of seriousness came over you. When off duty we often went to church in the city, either to No. 10 hospital or St. Peter's Episcopal church, where we heard the great organ from the gallery.

Amid the whirl and eddy of intense life and saddest death, we mingled with the garrison of Nashville, until the second day's fight at Stone River, when we were ordered to the front in charge of a wagon train loaded with supplies and ammunition for "Rosy's" army. Four companies of the regiment were on picket and we started at 11 a. m. for Murfreesboro, thirty miles distant, with six companies.

Eight miles from Nashville, when near the State Asylum, Wheeler's cavalry made a dash upon our train and had succeeded in destroying a few of the wagons in front, when a regiment of cavalry, sent back as an escort to our train, came up, and we drove the enemy into a cornfield, and they retreated southward.

CHAPLAIN A. L. PETTY.

Among the dead left by the enemy was a rebel officer, whose face was familiar. We searched and found a pass signed by General Thomas on which we had passed him many a time through the picket line on the Nolensville pike, near Nashville, as a gardener. Marching all night, we reached "Rosy's" army at three in the morning. We staid with the train until an ordnance officer relieved us, when we were ordered into line in the rear of Wagner's brigade on the left of Crittenden's line. Neither army was disposed to resume the offensive, and there was no hard fighting during the day. That night Bragg retreated and the battle of Stone River became a part of the history of the wicked rebellion.

The next day we returned to Nashville with an empty wagon train and resumed our former duties. Nashville was crowded with the sick and wounded of our army. After the battle, hospitals were established on every street, and in the endless procession of army trains coming into the city you might see a two-horse, canvas-covered wagon with very much the look of the vehicle that churns the pure country milk over the city pavements. Lashed to the side was the stretcher, two parallel shafts connected by a piece of sacking. These ambulances were a sort of flying hospital, carrying its burden of anguish, moving to and fro, free to go anywhere on the field of carnage.

Undertakers did a thriving business in Nashville. Coffins stood up on end, empty and hungry. They seem to petition you to get in and be composed. Here and there may be seen oblong, unpainted boxes, awaiting shipment, with the word *head* written on one end, and you think as I do that somebody is waiting for the lifeless form of one they loved in that home yonder.

These sad scenes make you forget the strange rivalry—as you meet mothers and wives with tear stained-faces, waiting to take home the dear dead boy or husband and bury him where they may visit his mound and strew it with flowers in all the years to come. Fathers, too, tremulous and sad, bear their boys back to the home they left, so brave and strong.

The regiment had become depleted by death and discharge, so that by April 7th we only reported a little over five hundred for duty. We lost from Sept 1st, 1862, to April, 1863, just one hundred by death in the hospitals, from disease alone. Seventy of them died in the Nashville hospitals between Dec. 1st, 1862, and April 20th, 1863. Many of those who died might have lived, could they have gone home, either on furlough or by discharge. Adjutant Charles H. Blackburn resigned about the first of December, '62, and 1st Lieut. Geo. A. Masury, of Company I, was appointed Adjutant, his commission dating from December 25th of the

T. H. MONTGOMERY, CO. G.

same year. Matthias Denman, who had filled the place of Adjutant's Clerk, died March 16th. Although he had been ailing for several weeks, he was absent from duty only a few days before his death. W. J. Funston of Company E, was detailed as Clerk and entered upon his duty a day or two before Comrade Denman's death.

Clerk Funston was surprised to find three discharge papers, which had been returned, approved, discharging the

the men from the service that they might reach home and mother, but alas, they looked and waited until hope ended in death.

These men died, discharged from the service by order of the General commanding, and those discharge papers had lain in the pigeon holes of the Adjutant's desk, from six to eight weeks, before their deaths occurred. It was all through the carelessness of the Adjutant. The like never occurred again.

April 7th we received our first pay as soldiers—five months, and the payment gave us seventy-two dollars and sixty-five cents, as our share—all in new crisp greenbacks and we were as proud of them as we were of the old flag we were fighting for. That night in our dreams we saw a large map of our country, stretched across the heavens from north to south. It was made of greenbacks, emblazoned on the map with letters of fire were the words *still united.* The dream was never forgotten. We had lost heavily in officers. Up to the middle of April eighteen had resigned and left the army, of the original field and company officers. Not one officer died of disease while in the service, ten were killed or died of wounds, and seventeen were wounded and survived the war, and one, Dr. Rosa, died from an overdose of morphine. He was found dead in his tent at McAfee Church, Georgia.

We moved out from Nashville twelve miles to Brentwood, and were glad to get away from the city. Our camp was on the little Harpeth river. The scenery would compare with the valleys through which the tributaries of the Hudson or Rhine flowed, and was beautiful "beyond description," as the novelist says. The 22nd Wisconsin and 19th Michigan had been captured here by Gen. Forrest a short time before.

Here we built a fort and spent two months of camp life, the most pleasant of all our army experience. The citizens,

—44—

unlike the country, were ugly, and rabid scessionists, displaying their hatred by occasionally firing on our pickets at night

The 52nd Regimental Band was organized shortly after we came to Brentwood. Lieut. James M. Summers of Company H, was active in its organization, and was its instructor. The following comrades were detached in its organization: David Brisbin, Co. A, leader; Jas. A Scott, Co. A, 2nd E flat cornet; John Baldwin, Co. I, 1st B flat; Hamilton Wallace, Co. G, 2nd B flat; Wm. Anshute Co. A, solo alto; Jerry Souders, Co. D, 1st alto; Burr Treat. Co. I, 2nd alto; Taylor Clark, Co. H, 1st tenor; George F. Irwin, Co. B, 2nd tenor; Jehu Peck, Co. D, baritone; Samuel Harper, Co. H. 1st bass; Hiram Rice, Co. K, tuba; J. M. Knisely Co. D, snare drum; Horace Church, Co. K, bass drum; T. McMasters, Co. B, tuba; Pinkney Bone, Co. B, cymbals; John Baldwin, bugler; J. M. Knisely, drum major. The band retained its organization with great credit to the regiment, until the close of the war.

CAPT. PARKER A. ELSON, CO. E.

CHAPTER IV.

While here Capt. J. T. Holmes received his commission as Major, to the satisfaction of the entire regiment. News came one evening announcing the fall of Richmond, and the camp was filled with excitement. All the candles, in the commissary were confiscated and cut in two. Expert climbers went into the tree tops, illuminating the branches with their flickering light. Huge bonfires were lighted and we shouted ourselves hoarse with joy, when Col Dan Mc-Cook arrived, reporting the news as "grape vine," while in reality the Union Army had been repulsed, was re-crossing the Rappahannock and retreating towards Washington.

Life at the front and life in the moon are very much alike. They were worlds without women, like your mother and mine. We cooked our beans and washed our clothes and swept the front of the tent, and wrote home saying "we are content and yet anxious". One night two comrades of the 125th Illinois, who were like David and Jonathan, inseparable, were on outpost duty on the Frank-lin pike. One of them who was in the habit of walking in his sleep, arose in the night and wandered across the line unseen by his comrade. Unheeding the challenge as he returned, he was shot and killed.

The weather was delightful during our stay at Brent-wood, and the health of the regiment excellent.

The second week of June we returned to Nashville and resumed our old duty of guarding trains or picketing. Shortly after out return to the city, a detail of five men from each regiment in the Brigade was made, and ordered to report at Division Headquarters in one hour.

It fell to our lot to report with four comrades at the adjutant's tent, for instructions, with orders to polish our shoes and brass mountings. We reported at division headquarters, where we were informed of our sad duty, the execution of a deserter, which was typical of the severe and inexorable character of the laws of war. The execution was to take place a mile south-west of our camp, and near the old Mason house, once occupied by Ex-President Polk.

In the squad detailed to execute the death penalty upon a comrade, there is always one musket loaded with a blank cartridge, so that each member of the detail may hope that he has fired the harmless shot. The condemned was a boy about 19 years of age, who had deserted from the 60th Ohio at Stone River. We waited for the ambulance bearing the unfortunate lad and his coffin. He was taken from the prison in the city and had just entered the ambulance when a dispatch was handed the officer in charge, bearing the signature of President Lincoln. It was a pardon, bringing joy to the condemned as well as relief to the executioners. The grave was filled and we returned to camp, feeling that surely there is but a step between us and death.

Rosecrans moved the 24th and we were ordered to the front, camping at Murfreesboro. Here we saw for the first time the "pup" tent. Over them were all kinds of odd signs, such as "No loafing," "A Baker," "Attorney at law, office upstairs." It was made in two sections or halves, fastened together with buttons. Each half was six feet by three, and had an improvised ridge pole, and two stakes with the cloth stretched and pinned down at the corners. The gable end was shut with a poncho, and the house was complete. When finished it resembled a chicken coop, and was christened a "Shelter Tent."

—48—

A short time before our trip to Murfreesboro, C. L. Vallandigham had gone through the lines, escorted by a body of cavalry, for disloyalty. The men on the outpost picket line told me, that no one knew who the stranger was, that was so carefully guarded. That was well enough, as it would not have been safe for him.

We passed the "Glorious Fourth" on picket near Murfreesboro. On returning the next morning to camp, we were entertained during the afternoon by a comic ballad singer He sang patriotic and other songs to the great delight of the boys, until some one started a report, that he was a rebel spy, and shouted "hang him" when he left camp in haste. In the evening, news came of the surrender of Vicksburg to Grant, with thirty thousand prisoners and one hundred guns, also that Meade had triumphed over Lee at Gettysburg. You may imagine we felt good from the crown of the head as far down as we went, manifesting our joy by "painting the town red." Our forces had captured Shelbyville and Tullahoma with many prisoners. We returned to Nashville, July 19, camping near the cemetery on College Hill, where we had an excellent view of the city.

There was great excitement in Ohio at this time, John Morgan had crossed the river and was sweeping through Southern Ohio, pursued by Gen. Shackleford's forces. How intensely we scanned the morning paper, and saw he was heading for the "old home" I had left about a year before. We quote from our diary July 24, "Morgan at Senecaville," July 25, "Morgan at Winchester; July 27, "In Jefferson County;" July 29, "Captured near Highlandtown."

Our camp had been occupied well nigh two years by the garrison troops, which had preceded us, so that its sanitary condition during the month of August, was very bad. We thought we were to be eaten up with vermin, such as rats, mosquitoes and flies, the old fashioned brown house fly—and you know what Burns spied on a lady's bonnet, and in his, "O wad some pow'r the giftie gie us To see oursels as ithers see us," endowe d it with immortality. All these follow the army. They are everywhere. The last named creature, against which, care and cleanliness are no adequate defense, is a superior production. Colonel Hinman in his history of the "Sherman Brigade" calls it by its scientific name "*Pediculus Vestimenti*," indicating its habit of browsing around upon the body and commends the use of this high sounding title, because it may be used in any company of polite people with comparative safety. Let us describe the creature. Equip a half macerated grain of wheat with a small detail of legs, say six or eight, a mouth and appetite and then draw a modest gray stripe along its back and you have the "famous gray-back," the crowning entomological triumph of the army It had no more respect for the deeply, darkly, beautifully blue of the officers than it has for the ragged blouse of the private And the only use made of its belongings was to throw its name at the next meanest creature encountered in the south, the "Johnny Reb."

But these were nature's scavengers and deserved protection. Look at the camp offices they performed, furnishing arguments for personal cleanliness, driving the soldier to soap and water, who could hardly be persuaded by a bayonet.

Every day some part of the regiment was sent as train guard to Stevenson, Alabama, one hundred and seventeen miles from Nashville. Usually from sixty to a hundred men were detailed and occupied a car, built so as to afford protection from the bushwhackers along the route. August 5th, a detail of seventy men, under command of Lieut. David Neighbor, started with a train, for the Tennessee river at Stevenson. It was early in the morning as we neared

Lavergne, running slowly on account of a dense fog, a train following us ran into the guard car, killing Obadiah and Levi Conwell, two brothers, and Elisha Wright, and severely injuring Lieut. David Neighbor by crushing his leg. All four of the comrades were from Company D

Col. D. D. Irons of the 86th Ill. died August 11th. He was greatly beloved by his men and chose to die in his tent,

CAPT. W. H. LANE, CO. E.

with the men he loved. We escorted the body to the Louisville and Nashville depot, from which it was sent to his home at Bloomington, Ill.

August 17 was an unlucky day for our guard. There were thirty-eight of us started before day for the front. The train was ditched by a torpedo, at Lavergne. The guards were attacked by bushwhackers, but were scattered by a volley from the car. In three hours we pulled out and everything seemed all right, until the engineer was shot at and so scared, that he pulled the lever wide open. Away we went, forty miles an hour, down grade, when the train left the track, again wrecking eleven of the nineteen cars, and injuring six of the guard. A train that followed us righted things and we doubled up the two trains, starting at two o'clock for Stevenson. On entering the long tunnel in the spur of the mountain, the rear engine gave out and the front one struggled to get us through. Black clouds of smoke rolled up and back to where we were lying on the top of a box car, the second from the tender. It grew denser and hotter, when like the Irishman, who was having a tooth extracted, "just before I died it pulled out."

On the morning of the 20th we marched south on the Franklin pike. On reaching the summit we looked back upon the city behind us, and bade farewell to all that was dear to us in Nashville,—"The Rock City"—having put our hand to the plough, and our faces turned toward the South. We never retraced our steps, nor have we ever set our feet within her gates, our fortune taking us, as we followed Thomas and Sherman with steady tread on bloody field and weary march to Chattanooga, and Atlanta, down to the sea and up through the Carolinas to Washington, home.

At Brentwood we halted for the night. That night Dick McCann, the noted bushwhacker, and eighteen of his men were decoyed into the picket line by the 14th Michigan, and captured, and poor Dick never carried a carbine again during the war. The second day brought us to Franklin, eighteen miles from Nashville. It is the county seat of Williamson county. At that time it had a population of one thousand. The town suffered much during the war, having been occupied many times by both armies, and was the scene of one of the hardest fought battles of the war, on

Nov. 30th, 1864, between the Union forces under Schofield, and the Rebel forces under Hood.

Gen. Schofield might have truly said, "My kingdom for a bridge", for that battle was fought to save Schofield's wagon trains, as the bridges over the Harpeth river had both been destroyed. Nearly all the able bodied men of Franklin were in the Confederate army and those at home were exceedingly bitter.

We tarried here two days. A large mass meeting was held during our stay, such as were held throughout the north during the campaign of 1863. The speakers were Andrew Johnson, the governor of Tennessee; Judge Brien; Col. McCook and Maj. J. T. Holmes. We were interested in Brownlow. He had preached and edited the "Knoxville Whig." The loyal people of East Tennessee believed in him next to the Bible. His recital of arrest and treatment at the hands of the Rebels was thrilling in the extreme.

Col. Dan told us that our sweethearts were looking for us home before Christmas, while Maj. Holmes eloquently spoke of the conflict for freedom and the right; how our arms had triumphed because our liberties are founded on Christian patriotism.

We passed through Columbia, the county seat of Maury county. It was at one time the capital of the state, also the residence of President Polk, before his election Our movements were slow, giving time for the repair of the railroad, as we expected to push supplies to the front by this line. We reached Linnville August 30th, camping near the spot where General Robert L. McCook had been murdered August 10th, 1862. He had become prostrated by a wound he had received at Mill Spring, Ky., which was followed by a severe attack of dysentery. He was lying on a bed in an ambulance which was driven along between two regiments of his division. A small band of guerrillas commanded by Frank Gurley, dashed out of the woods, and seeing the ambulance contained an officer of rank, who was lying on the bed undressed, asked who he was. Just then, the Federal troops coming in sight, they shot him as he lay and made good their escape.

Shortly after going into camp we were sent back to picket the rear, beyond the town of Linnville. In the morning as the assembly sounded in camp, our pickets were called in and the Captain detailed comrade, Joseph M. Thompson, and myself to fill a number of canteens at a spring, just outside the picket line. Returning we were fired upon by guerrillas, the same band that had murdered Gen. Mc-Cook, and both of us fell by the wayside, wounded.

The company came to our rescue, and, with the aid of mounted scouts, succeeded in capturing two of the band, who were taken to Nashville, tried and convicted of the murder of Gen. McCook and were hung. One of them made an address on the scaffold; declaring his innocence by saying, "I have never taken the life of any man."

Linnville was burned that morning, it being the home of the leader of the guerrilla band.

Our wounds were dressed and we were placed in an ambulance and taken through to Stevenson, Alabama, with the hospital tents and supplies. All day long the bushwhackers followed us, keeping up a continuous fire on our rear guard. Crossing the state line the next day at Boiling Spring, we were on Alabama soil. The country was rough and the people very poor. At Athens we struck the valley of the Tennessee, about twenty-five miles above the shoals.

We slept in the hospital tent. After breakfast we discovered we had a scorpion for a bedfellow. It had crawled under the blanket and there curled himself up as cozy as you please. The scorpion of the southern states is of the "genus bruchus" species—are small and their sting was often fatal.

Huntsville is twenty-two miles from Athens, which distance we marched in one day. It is the county seat of Madison county, Alabama, and is ten miles north of the Tennessee. It was a beautiful town, surrounded by the best of plantations, many northern capitalists having settled there before the war.

We pushed on to Stevenson, forty miles distance, in three days. The roads were rough, especially for wounded men. One of the springs of our ambulance was broken the second day, and we were jostled over the stones at a great rate. The next day we arrived at Bridgeport and there joined the first division of our corps, and the reserve corps, commanded by Gen. Gordon Granger.

Dr. Henry M. Duff, having been our family physician before the war, took me into his own mess and tent and we were not sent with the rest of the sick and wounded back to Nashville. While we lay at Bridgeport, Frank Duff the Hospital Steward, took us with him out into the country, so uth of the river, with an ambulance in search of milk and delicacies for the sick. We came to a cabin about five miles from the river on the Alabama side. The family seemed poor and ignorant. The old man talked freely. He seemed to think the country somewhat changed, but had no definite idea of the cause of the calamities that befel him and his neighbors. He had been told that a "feller named Abe Linkum had raised old Satan some hows and was ruinatin things, but he diden't know for certain. He had hearn that a feller was speakin round for Congriss or suthin, tellin the people to secesh and he heern they had seceshed. Thars suthin about the niggers in it, but weuns hav'nt got any niggers and don't know much about it. Of course we could get salt and things if it wasn't for them abbilisheners. These

—55—

were substantially the words of the old man—a specimen of the "white trash" of the south before the war. They had been falsely educated and believed that Lincoln was the author of all the woes that befell the south. The people of Northern Alabama were very poor and had the least possible communication with the outer world. The women were clothed in the coarsest fabrics, spun on hand wheels and woven on rude domestic looms, such as are found today as souvenirs of the backwood's cabin. Pitiful to the last degree, was the condition of the country with its starving, rudely clad mothers and abandoned wives, unwashed, uncombed, unattended children. The soil was poor, so poor that a comrade who had lost his way one night inquired at a cabin, of an old man, who came to the door, "how far it was to Brill's Ferry"? He found the old man's voice was so weak that it was impossible to hear him and inquired; what is the matter with your voice?" "The ground is too poor to raise my voice—can't raise anything but an umbrella down hur," replied the old man.

We moved on towards Chattanooga, marching all day, and camped at sundown at the foot of shell mountain. A bear cub was seen by the 86th, Ill. boys, on the picket line and was followed up the mountain and captured. Hungry and tired, we lay us down to sleep and soon all was quiet At eleven o'clock we were routed and ordered to be ready to march in twenty minutes These were times to try men's souls and tempers too, but at it we went, arriving at Chattanooga just before day light.

JOHN C. BROWN, CO. E.

CHAPTER V.

MORNING dawns and we have nothing for breakfast, no wagons or knapsacks. We ask each other, how long this is to last, but our eyes feast upon the scene before us. Stand by me, as I stood that beautiful September morning, near McCook's headquarters watching the mists clear away. The horizon all around rises and falls, like the waves of the sea. Stretching along the east and following to the south-west, you see the undulating ridge, edged with a thin fringe of trees. That is Mission Ridge, and you are looking upon what is to be the theatre of future battles. Looking south, Lookout Mountain is before you, grim and grand. Glorious glimpses of five states may be seen by those who stand upon its summit, but this is denied us just now. Within this sweep of grandeur lies a thing whose name shall endure, when yours and mine shall have been forgotten. It is the town of Chattanooga. Before war's fingers had clutched it, there was one main business street to give to it a little commercial pulsation; residences, some of them beautiful, a few of them stately. A stunted, rusty looking market house, four or five churches of indifferent fashion, two or three hotels, whose entertainment has de parted, and a few low tenement houses are about all there is of the city for which we are contending.

As you pass along the central street, the dingy signs of old dead business catch the eye, where "A Long, Attorney at law," once uttered oracles and tobacco juice, federal stores have taken place of law books. Where ribbons and laces ran smoothly over the salesman's fingers, the cot of the sick and the quiet step of the nurse may be seen and heard. Fences have gone up in camp fires. Tents are pitched like mushrooms in the flower beds, and gardens are occupied as mule pens. Such was Chattanooga as we saw it on the morning of September 13, 1863.

Upon the sidewalks is a procession of blue coats all day, and you may look and not see one woman of the noble race that put men upon their honor and make the world braver and purer. The Southern aristocracy had fled with the rebel army. To be sure, you may see many an "Aunt Chloe," dressed in turban, like a sooty chimney, red hot at the top. And there, too, is a colorless native, a woman that had come down from the mountains, dressed in white, unwashed, uncrinolined, unflounced. When I saw her, she had come to the post office, expecting to get a letter from her husband, who had been conscripted into the rebel army. When informed that no mail came from the rebel army, she stood in front of the building, the picture of sadness, and seemed to be meditating on what she would do, all the while spitting at a mark, a nail head, and tobacco juice at that. A few hours in such a place as that made one think of home, of peace and plenty. That condition was possible before the war. There were white as well as black slaves, and that conflict redeemed the poor whites as well as the enslaved blacks.

Chattanooga had less than four thousand population when Bragg left with his army and rebel sympathizers. It is situated on the Tennessee river one hundred and fifty miles from Nashville by rail. The river was navigable as far as Knoxville. We reached Rossville Gap, September 14th. The wagon train did not reach us, and we were necessarily thrown on our own resources. It was "root hog or die." Our Col. Dan said, "Get to the woods boys and keep out of sight." The boys kept coming in all day with meat and forage of all kinds, necessary to satisfy a hungry soldier. Gen. Gordon Granger, who was in command of the reserve corps, of which we were now a part, began to arrest the foragers and by four o'clock had quite a number of them tied up by the thumbs with cords stretched over the limb of a tree, in front of his tent.

Our men fell in and marched with fixed bayonets column in front to the General's tent, without an officer, and demanded the release of the men who were being punished. The General in a rage ordered a section of our own Battery, the 2nd. Illinois commanded by Capt. Barnett to open fire with blank cartridge on the complainants, then if they did not disperse, with grape and canister. But the battery refused to move to a man. The cords were cut by our men and they quietly moved back to their quarters. The officers of the regiment were ordered to deliver up their swords, but the battle of Chickamauga coming on in a few days the whole matter was lost sight of. One thing that seemed to indicate to us that Gen. Granger was afraid of the outcome of his severity in discipline was the temporary transfer of our Brigade from the reserve corps to Gen. Steadman's Division in the first day's fight at Chickamauga.

On the evening of September 17, the three corps of the Army or the Cumberland, for the first time in three months, were in supporting distance of each other. The left rested at Rossville Gap, the right at Steven's Gap, beyond Lafayette. Rosecran's force was about sixty thousand, but a fair estimate of our forces engaged at Chickamauga is fifty-two thousand. Wagner's Brigade held Chattanooga, and Post's was guarding the trains and were not engaged. According to the most reliable data obtainable since the war, Bragg's aggregate force was over eighty thousand. Bragg's right was near Lee and Gordon's mill, and his left near Lafayette.

CAPT. S. M. NEIGHBOR, CO. D.

Longstreet's corps coming to Dalton by rail road, was to cross at the bridges and fords below the mill, and, if possible drive the whole army up the valley, and thus get between our forces and Chattanooga. Dan McCook's Brigade was posted at Reed's bridge on the morning of the first day's fight. Early in the morning our men captured a number of prisoners that proved to be from Longstreet's corps, which had just arrived from Richmond. The battle of Chickamauga was opened that morning by our pickets, as at Perryville, and the bridge was stubbornly held, until late in the afternoon, when the rebel General Bushrod Johnson affected a crossing. Our mounted troops saved Crittenden's corps on the first day, by their resistance of the enemies approach to our lines. The opening skirmish began for the possession of a spring between the pickets of the 52nd, and the enemy, which was the beginning of the historic battle of Chickamauga.

Our brigade was thrown on the extreme left of the line in the second day's battle, except late in the afternoon, when we were moved out on the line near the Snodgrass house, and were fortunate in not being driven from our position when darkness came on. Our loss was light, only seventeen killed and wounded.

During the night the 86th Ill. covered the retreat of Rosecran's army, until within the trenches around Chattanooga. It was the most fiercely contested battle of the war. Gen. John B. Gordon in his lecture on "The last days of the Confederacy" labors to prove that Chancellorsville was the hardest fought battle of the war. Those who have gone over the Chickamauga battlefield and saw the undergrowth of timber, almost entirely shot away, can have some idea of the storm of lead necessary to produce such results. The ordnance officer of McCook's corps, says "That one hundred and four wagon loads of bullets alone were fired at the "Johnny's" by that corps, at Chickamauga.

Astounding as this statement may seem, it does not give one so clear an idea of the amount of lead shot away in a battle, as the statement of Mrs. Snodgrass, around whose house the storm of battle raged, Sunday afternoon, September 20th. In answer to the question as to how the battle affected her financially, she said, that everything was destroyed and that she and her children would have suffered, had it not been for the lead they had gathered from the battlefield. She also said, that they had gathered hundreds of pounds of bullets, which they sold in Chattanooga, at five and six cents per pound, and that this crop did not fail them for some years.

I was left in Hospital No. 3 in Chattanooga while the battle was fought, not being fully recovered from the wounds received at Linnville, Tennessee.

I saw not the charge and counter charge, but I saw the deadly work, the blood and carnage. On the morning of the first day's battle the wounded began to arrive. The surgeons laid off the green sash and coat, rolled up their sleeves, spread out the terrible glitter of steel, and made ready for work. The wounded came in slowly at first, one man nursing a shattered arm, another and another lying here and there, waiting his terrible turn. The work goes right on, arms are lopped off like slips of golden willow, feet, that never turned from the foe, forever more without an owner, strew the ground.

Knives are busy and saws play. It is a bloody work. The surgeon who does his work well, is a prince among men. Cool and calm, quick and tender, he feels among the arteries and fingers the tendons as if they were harp strings. A poor fellow writhes and a smothered moan escapes him. "Be patient my boy," says the surgeon cheerfully, I'll make you all right in a minute." It was a right arm that was to come off at the elbow and the boy slipped off a ring, that clasped the poor useless finger that was soon to blend with Tennessee soil, and put it in his pocket. Another sits up while the surgeon follows the bullet that has buried itself in his side. "George," said a comrade, who was starting home on a furlough, to one who had been mangled by several shots, "What shall I tell them at home for you?" "Tell them," said he, "that there is hardly enough of me left to say I, but hold down here a minute, "Tell Kate there is enough of me left to love her still."

Such scenes as these were witnessed every day in the hospital, and such everywhere followed the battle. Many of those seriously wounded fell into the hands of the enemy, and the worst cases were paroled. I. S. Winters, of Co. I, 40th Ohio, fell in a charge by a canister ball lodging in the fleshy part of the leg below the knee. As he lay on the field in the sun, he took his knife from his pocket, cut out the ball, was paroled and lived to preach a number of years after the war.

During the night of September 21st, the army of the Cumberland was withdrawn from the lines at Rossville, to

Chattanooga.   Our brigade and a brigade of regulars were left to hold the breast works until after midnight.   At one time the brigade of regulars became panic stricken and ran over our lines.   Col. Dan was very angry and cursed them as cowards.   When all had passed, we, too, marched silently away after the main body.   The union loss is officially stated at 1,641 killed, 9,262 wounded and 4,945 prisoners. The Confederate reports are wanting.

JOHN I. CABLE, CO. A.

CHAPTER VI.

OUR STAY AT NORTH CHICKAMAUGA.

LONGSTREET never reported his losses, but the entire loss was not far from 18,000, while our own was 15,-851. The enemy advanced slowly, taking possession of Missionary Ridge and the valley between the ridge and Lookout Mountain, also the mountain, picketing the south bank of the river to Bridgeport, compelling our wagon trains to come to Stevenson by way of Jasper, cross the Sequatchie valley and Waldron's Ridge, a distance of 58 miles from the terminus of railroad facilities, and completely blockading the river in the use of boats. The possession of Chattanooga was of great importance to the north, both as a base for further advances and as the key to loyal East Tennessee. When the battle was over our army had ten days' rations and ammunition enough to last two days' hard fighting, while on the defensive, earth-works grew like "Jonah's gourd," yet we were in a tight place—*bottled up.* The Brigade camped in the cemetery until the 25th, when we crossed the river and moved up the river eight miles to the mouth of North Chickamauga, camping at Caldwell's Ford

It had not rained for some time and the river and creek were very low, but the water was very clear and pure. We built heavy fortifications along the line of the river and felt that another move would not be made soon, as neither army was in the condition to take the offensive. From our camp we had a fine view of Lookout Mountain, now occupied by the rebels, who seemed to say, "If we cannot whip you, we can look down upon you." With the October winds came the long looked for rain and Oh! how it did rain. It rained all day, and it rained all night. One evening we were relieved from the picket line by the 86th Ill. Dark came on and we started for camp. We lost our way in the darkness, the creek was very high and the temporary bridge had been swept away. We put up in an old log building for the night. The next morning we came upon an old homestead, standing where once a garden smiled. The fences were gone, the grounds black and bare, the meaning of the word *desolation*, not be be found in the lexicon, could be seen on the face of all these regions, and the people only added human intensity to the picture, for they looked like men and women whose almanac was a fragment; people without a tomorrow. If there is anything in the world more desolate, I have yet to see it. A poor old horse was feebly grazing, near by a man sat in the doorway, gazing vacantly at the scene before him, stripped of all, garner empty, fields unsown. The little band had wandered away, and now he came all alone that day to linger around that home he loved. As we looked at him, we said, "If God does not always temper the wind to the shorn lamb," he sometimes blesses the creature with thorough endurance.

Election day came October 13th. By a law passed the winter before, Ohio soldiers were allowed to vote. It had been one of the most exciting campaigns ever known at home, but all was quiet in the army. The voting was conducted in the same manner as elections at home. The contest for Governor was between John Brough and C. L. Vallandigham. The regiment cast 338 votes, 327 of these for Brough, and eleven for Valandigham. Our company cast 39, all of which were for Brough. Fourteen were under age, showing that we had fifty-three men able for duty in the company, and four hundred and seventy-two in the regiment. The army was reorganized. Rosecran's was relieved, and Gen. Thomas put in command. McCook and Crittenden were both relieved. The old Twentieth and Twenty-first were consolidated and called the Fourth, Gen. Granger in command. We were assigned to the 14th corps with Gen. Jeff. C. Davis as division commander. We are now in the 3rd Brigade, 2nd Division, 14th Army corps.

Our condition and prospects grew worse and worse. The roads were in such a state, that the wagons were eight days in making the journey from Stevenson to Chattanooga, and one time there were five hundred teams halted between the mountain and the river, unable to pull through for want of forage for the animals. The artillery horses were dying so fast that batteries could not have moved under any circumstance. Men working on the fortifications, shouted "crackers" at the officers as they passed. All kind of schemes were practiced to get rations. Enlisted men would purchase in the name of a commissioned officer, and when the latter applied, he would be told, that he had already received his allowance. We were part of the time on quarter rations. I have eaten three days' rations for breakfast and dinner, and skirmished round for the other seven meals, and have gone to the butcher pens and scraped the beef hides for material, out of which to make soup. Prof. Leibig said, "a man who eats beef, and another who eats bread, view a difficulty from an entirely different standpoint, that a man's dinner flies into his head by the same sign that it goes into the stomach, and that what he eats makes thought as well as muscle. So to know a people thoroughly you must either examine their larder, smell their chimney smoke, or stroll through their market." I wonder how the Professor would carry out his theory in our camp, for we were actually starving. We did steal the corn from the mules, and the mules and horses starved by the thousands, as every man in the army of the Cumberland knows that Sherman had to bring up horses to move the artillery of our army at Mission Ridge. The trees were barked everywhere by the hungry animals. Men thought they heard the train coming with relief, but it was only the sough of the wind among the mountains. The bridge, the bridge. was all their thought. Their faces grew fixed; there

W. J. McCANN. CO. E.

was but one anxious expression on them all. They lifted up their eyes and saw Bridgeport and Stevenson and Nashville filled with army stores, while famine stared them in the face. They were like men athirst in the desert, for whom the magic of the mirage lifts the clear waters with their cool margins of green and mocks with the shadow of blessing their dry and dying eyes. At last Hooker came with fifteen thousand men from the east, and Lookout valley was opened up and when his cannon began to roar the boys said, "Hooker is opening up our cracker line", so he did, bringing our supplies thirty-one miles nearer, and we took a long breath, for the pioneer of great joy had come and we had plenty again. But the boys had many things to be thankful for. We had unbounded confidence in "Pap Thomas," who had said to Grant, "We'll hold Chattanooga, if we starve.

Again there was seldom an exchange of shots, between the pickets. Very few men were shot from Oct. to Nov.

2oth.   And still another thing gave no cause for complaint—the boys found some way to get their tobacco.   You could always tell when a boy was out of tobacco, especially on picket.   Everything would smoke on the train, from the engine to the axle.   The negroes would sing and pray pat juba, or dance for tobacco.   In Northern Alabama the women chew and smoke.   Picture one of these women, guiltless of reading, writing, soap, water or religion, who says "you uns" and "we uns," with a piece of tobacco in her mouth and two or three children at her heels, and you have the counterfeit presentiment of a type of white folks, fairly pushed over the edge of decent existence.   They grew up in the mountain country of the south.   Most of them indulged in the luxury called "dipping".   Take a stem of sassafras, chew it into a bit of a broom at one end, dip it in snuff and sweep your mouth with it, leave the handle sticking out of one corner, like a broom in a mop pail, and you have as much of the fashion as I mean to describe.   We had a sample of the eastern army in Hooker's men, and saw them tested afterwards in many a hard-fought battle.

The first week in November, Longstreet left our front with his corps and Wheeler's cavalry to drive Burnside from Knoxville.   We returned from Lookout Valley to our old camp at North Chickamauga and began fixing up our quarters for winter.   There was no change at the front.   We carefully guarded the river, occasionally throwing a shot over from our battery to keep the "Johnnies" awake.   We were paid off on Sunday the 15th.   The rebels were throwing an occasional shell at us, and we thought, perhaps, the paymaster was desiring to get away from the danger.   They tried to scare us on the morning of the 17th by shelling our camp, killing Chaplain Levi Sanders of the 125th Ill., he being the only man injured.

We asked one of the 125th boys, a few days afterwards, why the Chaplain was the only man touched, and he said,

"I suppose he was the only man in the regiment that was prepared to die."

Recruiting Sergeants were sent home to fill up the depleted ranks. Very few were on the sick list. While our camp duties kept us out of mischief, many strange incidents occurred while we camped here that cannot readily be forgotten. One of the companies had a boy, who vowed he would not have his hair cut while the war lasted. One evening, on dress parade the Colonel ordered the Captain to make a detail and cut his hair close to the scalp. The detail was made and the comrade was held down on the Company street, while his head was stripped of his shaggy locks, in the presence of the whole regiment.

It was at North Chickamauga that a guard fell asleep while sitting on the top of a pile of corn that had been pulled with the husks on. When three companies of the regiment had carried away two-thirds of the corn, Volney Blue, of Company F, slid head-foremost to the ground, and awoke to find himself within a few feet of Maj. Holme's tent, and his guarded treasure gone. The next morning, every tent was searched and not an ear of corn found. Nov. 20th, Gen. Bragg sent in a note requesting the removal of non-combatants from the city. Grant had arrived and fearing that Bragg might slip away, either to escape battle or push through by Knoxville into Kentucky, ordered Thomas to move out and force the enemy to develop their lines. We laid quietly in our camp until after midnight of the morning of the 24th, when we were ordered to assist Gen. Sherman in crossing the river above the enemy's right. One hundred and sixty canvass row boats were quietly launched in the bend of the creek. Gen. Giles A. Smith's brigade was the first to enter the boats, the 52nd Ohio and 86th Ill. furnishing the oarsmen. Five oarsmen and twenty-five armed men in each boat, floated silently down into the Tennessee and down that stream, crossing at a designated point above the mouth of South Chickamauga creek where two regiments landed and, moving quietly, captured all the enemy's pickets, taking the officer of the day out of his bed in a house near by. Meanwhile the flotilla dropped down below the mouth of the creek, landed the other regiments of the brigade, and at once rowed back to the north shore for another load. By day-light, on the morning of the 24th, 8,000 men, two divisions, were on the south bank and covered by a strong rifle trench.

The pioneer corps at once began to throw a pontoon bridge, 1,350 feet long across the Tennessee, and another across South Chicamauga creek. Both bridges were completed before noon. Providence favored us with a heavy fog, and the mist about the city and Lookout enabled a small steamboat, the "Dunbar," to ferry some of Sherman's horses across, to be used in moving Thomas's artillery, as his horses were so nearly starved they were unable to move the batteries. Our division, Jeff. C. Davis', crossed on the bridge.

PETER GIFFEN, CO. F.

CHAPTER VII.

MISSION RIDGE AND RELIEF OF BURNSIDE.

GRANT had intended making the attack the day before, but the delay was unavoidable and lamented. If I may say so, the wheels upon their axles had been rusted by the rain, and the machine was motionless. What a strange problem is a battle, dependent sometimes upon a breath of wind or a drop of water. All day the rebel lines were restless. Trains and brigades passing and repassing, like the sliding pictures in a magic camera. There was a fearful looking for of coming judgment. The work of landing the troops on the other side had kept us from our rest for two nights, and we stacked arms in the rear of Grant's headquarters, which was in the rear of Orchard Knob. The knob was a conical mound, perhaps a hundred feet high, once wooded, but now bald. In front of it were ledges of rock and a rolling sweep of open ground for two miles or more, and seemed to dash against Mission ridge, that lifts itself like a sea wall, eight hundred feet high. It was wooded, rocky, precipitous and wrinkled with ravines. On the top of that wall were the rebels and their batteries. Below the first pitch, three hundred feet down are more rebel batteries, and still below are their camps and rifle pits.

At one o'clock, twenty five hundred yanks were in line, led by a line of skirmishers. You should have seen that line, two miles long, as straight and unwavering as a ray of light. On they went, driving in the pickets before them. On the summit of Mission Ridge, a little to the south-east of Fort Wood, was a cluster of buildings. Gen. Grant is viewing them with a field glass, and he tells his chief of staff that there is a gray horse ready saddled at the door, it is the headquarters of Braxton Bragg. Gen. Hooker pushed his lines round Lookout and up the slopes, fighting all day and until one o'clock in the night. A curtain of cloud was hung around the mountain all day by the God of battles, even our God. It was the veil of the temple, that could not be rent. Friend and foe were wrapped in a seamless mantle and two hundred would cover our entire loss, while our brave mountaineers strewed the mountain with four hundred dead, and 1,000 prisoners. The 40th Ohio leaped over their works, as the wicked twin Roman leaped over his brother's mud wall, capturing their artillery with a Mississippi regiment and gaining a point on the summit. This is the story of Joe Hooker "fighting above the clouds", and it was true. When Lookout was captured, Hooker and his men were far above the cloud mist that enveloped the mountain. We, in the valley, never witnessed a grander sight. The flash of the guns was like the play of lightning in the heavens above us. It was Sinai over again, with its thunderings and lightnings and thick darkness, and we knew the Lord was on our side, and when the thunder began to roll around Lookout, we stood as almost in the presence of the God of the whole earth. The afternoon is half gone, and Grant for the first time shows signs of restlessness. His hour had come. The north and the south are marshalling for a great conflict. A hundred thousand witnesses cover the hive sloped hills. It is the most solemn congregation that ever stood in the presence of the God of battles. The signal guns are firing. Out moves the skirmish line and after them the splendid columns. They charged to the first rifle pits with a cheer, forked out the foe with the bayonets and lay there, panting for breath. The enemy opened all along the line. It was rifles and musketry, it was grape and canister, it was shot and shell. Mission Ridge had been the sounding-board for Chickamauga before. The old army of the Cumberland had been there—it is here. It is said that the men did not wait for orders to charge the Ridge. Look and you see the most startling episode of the war. The men are up, Sheridan with his hat on the point of his sword, is saluting the enemy and making for the hill like a bold riding hunter. They go up, up to the crest. See those banners that were borne at Pea Ridge, bathed in blood at Ft. Donnelson, glorified at Stone River, waved at Shiloh, and riddled at Chicakmauga. Three times the flag of the 27th Ill. goes down and, *you know why, three* color sergeants lie between the base and the summit. But the flag is immortal, it comes up again and the regiment moves on. How sublime was the thunder of the artillery; it was like the foot of God on the mountain side. Just as the sun, weary of the scene, was sinking out of sight, and we were wishing for some Joshua to stay its course, that invincible army swept over the crest, and the day was ours. As we went up with Sherman to the left, we looked, and that *old flag* was there. The routed hordes rolled off to the north and east, like a worn out storm cloud. Bragg, who ten minutes before was putting his men back into the rifle pits, rode off into Dixie, at a "two-forty," gait. On Monday before, he had said the Yankees would leave Chattanooga in five days. They left in three days by way of Mission Ridge, straight over the mountains as, their fathers did.

But the scenes on that hill top can never be painted. As our boys surged over the rebel works, cheer after cheer, rang like bells, through the valley of the Chickamauga. Men flung themselves, exhausted, on the ground. They laughed, they wept, they shook hands and embraced each other, then turned around and did the same thing again. It was as wild as a carnival. A little German boy was pierced like the lid of a pepper box, but is neither dead nor wounded: "see here, captain, see here, a pullet hit the preech of my gun, a pullet in my pocket book, a pullet in mein coat tail, dey shoots me, tree, five times, and, mine Gott; I'se all right yet." How that old East Tennesseean, who gave us such a welcome, got there, nobody knows, but there he was, grasping our hands and saying "I knew you Yanks would fight." Up behind Mission Ridge rose the silver moon, for it was full that night. No blood in it, for the earth drank it up, and by eight o'clock all was quiet. It was a great victory.

FIRST LIEUT. ALEXANDER SMITH, CO. E.

Fifty-two pieces of artillery, 10,000 stands of arms, 7,000 prisoners, yet I could not roll the burden from my heart. All these would not bring back to life the brave men who fell in achieving it. More men fell in that battle, with whom I had been acquainted, than any other battle of the war. Let that struggle be known as the battle of Missionary Ridge, suggestive of the great mission of freedom. And now, as the calmer days of peace have come, and the north and south have joined in commemorating that struggle, in monuments to their dead, and annually make a pilgrimage to those battlefields, and greet each other under "Old Glory," they will need no guide to conduct them to the spot where the battle raged.

Rust may have eaten the guns; the graves of the dead may have been opened and the bones removed; the soldier and his leader may lie down together, but there stands Mission Ridge, a fitting monument, and there it will stand forever. We started in pursuit of the rebels, early next morning, in the direction of Gray's Station on the Knoxville railroad. The enemy made a stand in the edge of a meadow, fringed with a heavy growth of underbrush. We were deployed as skirmishers. A minnie ball struck the blade of a small hatchet, which we carried in our belt, bending the blade, but saving our life. We charged them, capturing a number of prisoners and part of their wagon train. A wagon load of tobacco was distributed among those who used the narcotic. Knoxville was besieged by Longstreet, and we set out to relieve Burnside, who was in command of the forces, marching eighteen to twenty-five miles a day, without overcoats. Many of our men were almost barefooted. One of my shoes was almost gone. Henry H. Scott and I drew a pair between us. He took the right shoe, and I mated the left, and thus we fared much better than many of the company. The government was abundantly able to clothe her soldiers, but was over three hundred miles from her base of supplies, with but one line of communication and that frequently raided by the enemy. The wonder is that we fared as well as we did. With two days' rations when we left Chickamauga, we lived off the country, until we halted, nine miles from Knoxville, at Ganley's Mills, at the junction of the Connassauga and Hiawassie rivers. Longstreet gave up the siege, and retreated toward Lynchburg, Va. Capt. Hutchinson was a miller by trade, and made the old mill hum, running it day and night, grinding corn and buckwheat, and we fared better for a while. Here we found unmistakable signs of loyalty to the old flag. Women and children were as false to the south as fathers, brothers and sons were, and woe to the rebel soldier, who was recognized as such, who followed paths into which he was guided by these loyalists. The people were poor. They read the Bible and Parson Brownlow's Whig and death to all enemies of the Union was their watchward. The bushwhacker's definition of war was written accurately in tears and blood and flame.

While camping at the mill near the Chilhouri Mountain, in company with Lieut. Miser, Joe Swan and Benton Wilson, the Colonel's hostler, with three comrades from Co. E., we went out in search of forage for the horses. A few miles out, we separated, Lieut. Miser, Swan and the colored boy going up the valley, while we turned down the stream. The Lieut. and his party succeeded in finding a still-house and filled their canteens. Stopping at a farm house, they awaited dinner. We will let Benton tell their adventure in his quaint way. They left him out in the road to watch. He says—"I was standing by the gate talking to a yaller gal when she startled me with the cry, 'Dere comes de rebs.' I jumped de fence, run through de house hollerin' "de rebs is a comin', but de poor Lieut. and Swan, dey had too much of de still-house and didn't hear me. De rebs saw me a makin' for de mountain and shouted 'Halt dere'—but I didn't halt. I jist took de wings of de mornin' and flew up de mountain and dey didn't catch dis nigger. But poor Lieut. and Joe, were captured. Dey were to full to heah me." Kimbrough's bushwhackers took them prisoners, with three good horses. The men had borrowed Major Holme's brace of pistols that they might be ready for an emergency, and these were gone. Maj. Holmes sent a detachment of troops eight or ten miles across the mountain and brought in Kimbrough's father as a hostage, and brought the son to time.   In a few days, the men and three horses were exchanged for the father, the only loss being the brace of pistols.   We turned down the valley and found a house where we waited for dinner.   While waiting, a breathless, excited colored boy came running into the house and said, "Missus de yanks is comin' down dar in de road, and dere won't be nary a chicken left 'fore night on de place," and Joe rubbed his hands together, grinned and twisted his body, and giving me a nod, went out.   Suspecting trouble, we followed him.   "Dere's no yanks heah abouts, but you'd better look out for dem whackers over de hill, I saw some dis mornin'."   I asked Joe what he intended to do when he was set free.   "I dunno marsa," he answered, "but I'se gwine to sleep in de sunshine, wrapped up in pancakes, an yaller gal angels dere will pour lasses ober me."   This was a a heavenly picture of perfect negro beatitude and its realization was near at hand.   Taking Joe's hint of danger near, we gathered up what our haversacks would hold and struck for camp.

Dec. 15th we broke camp in East Tennessee, starting back to Chattanooga.   The weather was stormy and we suffered for shelter and food.   We had left Mission Ridge after the battle for the relief of Burnside but three weeks before. The day we started was Thanksgiving, and we were happy as we could be.   We had moved in light marching order, without baggage wagons.   Now, on our return from that excursion, the hardest line of privations we suffered during the war came.   Wet and shivering, the soldiers trudged along by day through the mud, churned by the tread of countless feet, but when night came, we crept under our cheerless pup tents, often with only brush or rails to keep our chilled bodies from the cold, sodden ground.   Crossing the Tennessee at Chattanooga at mid-night, on the ferry, we marched

JOHN SMITH, CO. D.

to our old camp on North Chickamauga, finding everything as we left it four weeks before. The work of improve-
ment goes briskly on. We think we are to stay here all winter.
Plenty of clothing, plenty of rations, no parched corn or beef
tripe. How unlike the weeks spent here when Bragg
watched the almost empty pot boil over the slow camp fire.

Christmas came, but a soldier's Christmas was like other
days. Even the Chaplain seemed to have forgotten the day
and nothing occurred. We did not hang up our stockings,
but they were full in the morning, because we slept with
them on. Our dinner consisted of hardtack, bacon, coffee
and bean soup. Speaking of Chaplains, you ask me how
about their work and efficiency. The Chaplaincy at best
was an office difficult and thankless, demanding the best
men to fill it well and worthily. Men whose presence and
bearing put soldiers upon their honor, and it is safe to say,
that he who was fit to be a Chaplain, was fit to rule a people.
Two-thirds of the Chaplains who failed, were without back-
bone to assert their rights with the officers of the regiment.
I have known a Colonel to call out the regiment on Sunday
dress parade, during the religious services of the Chaplain,
and because he remonstrated, was put under a ban at headquarters. Many of them were efficient. There was that old
loyal hearted Lyon of the 85th Ill. Well equipped with a
heart and no head to speak of. A pure man. I used to
think the regiment grew daily worse. They asked him to
resign a day or two before the battle of Kenesaw. On the
day of the charge he carried water to the men all day. In
the hottest places there was the old bronzed face of this man
of God, and the bond between the Chaplain and the men was
sealed on that field, which will hold good to the end of their
lives. Chaplain McFarland of the 97th Ohio was a minister
of mercy. Verily, I say unto you he has his reward. Nobody could tell tonight where he will be tomorrow, and yet

with the morning's dawn, the camp is astir, and the preparation began for staying all winter. The cozy little cabins, begun before the battle of Mission Ridge, were finished and neatly fitted up, adorned and ready. A fire-place is artistically constructed and plastered with the inevitable red earth. A crane is hung in it, no one knows where it came from, a dinner pot adorns the crane and the whole interior presents a genuine homelike air. A bit of looking glass against the wall. A substitute for carpet marks the stepping-off place for the land of dreams. Snugly fixed in just such a snug little cabin, my mess mate, Tommy Thompson, and I settled down in peace, when just before tattoo, Christmas night, down comes an order to march at five in the morning. No complaints, no murmurings, no watching out the night. Every bundle of a blanket has a sleeping soldier in it. Every knapsack has a drowsy head upon it. At four, bugle calls to breakfast. The camp is awake. A drizzling rain has set in, but unusual fires are built, for the wood must be cleaned up. "Be ready to start at five," shouts the sergeant major. Tents are struck, knapsacks packed, wagons loaded, mules harnessed, all is ready. Soldiers have notions, and among them are the destruction of improvements. The cottages are in flames, and the stools and tables are reduced to glowing coals, and if they don't fiddle as Nero did while their Rome is burning, they are having a jolly time of it, with their fun and jokes. It was a dingy morning, when the brigade marched out of camp with a good cheer, the army wagons streaming and swearing after us, we are bound for—we don't know where We looked back upon that old camp, leaving nothing behind but empty desolation. Will you wonder if I tell you that I have watched with a pang of regret that old camp, worn smooth and beautiful by the touch of brave feet, whose owners have trod upon thorns with song? Feet —alas! how many of them in all this coming and going world, will ever make music again on the old threshold? How many such sights of perished cities that war made, and how many bonds of good fellowship have been rent to be reunited no more? Oh, how many memories came crowding in upon us as we left that old camp. It was there we had the "blues," so bad at times, that some of the boys are spotted yet. There, where we gathered about the towering cliffs of Lookout more than three months before, when all the future was wrapped in doubt.

CAPT. A. C. THOMAS, CO. C.

CHAPTER VIII.

WE cross the Tennessee at Chattanooga, go over Missionary Ridge, camping at McAfee Church. The brigade, in the absence of Col. McCook was commanded by Col. Harmon, and the Division by Gen. Jeff C. Davis. Here we began to fix up for the winter, the companies being divided into messes of from six to ten men, with a captain to each mess. We immediately set to work erecting a log shanty to winter in. It rained three days, then turned cold. The night before New Year's was memorable as the coldest night ever known in the north. Many places the mercury went down to forty degrees below zero, while we thought it went to the bottom, in camp. Part of the mess kept up the fire while the rest slept. In the morning we found canteens, that had been filled with water, that were frozen and bursted.

The New Year came in cold and dreary, while we suffered greatly for want of shelter. A proclamation had been read offering $400 bounty and thirty days' furlough to all veterans who would re-enlist. One hundred and forty thousand re-enlisted during the month of January from the veteran regiments. Three hundred of these tried veterans were worth more than a thousand raw recruits to Sherman's army.

On the morning of the 6th, Dr. A. J. Rosa, assistant surgeon of the regiment, was found dead in his tent. He suffered greatly from neuralgia, and on retiring had taken a dose of morphine from which he never wakened. He was a quiet faithful officer, respected by all.

We moved six miles south of McAfee, February 14th, camping near Lee and Gordon's Mills, where we began the life of a soldier in earnest, drilling four hours a day, policing camp and picketing.

The regiment received eighty-seven recruits, filling up the depleted companies of the regiment, giving us 578 able for duty. These recruits had to be drilled, and we were at it every day. One morning as we were returning from Chattanooga, we had the pleasure of witnessing our division on drill. Old fashioned Jimmy D. Morgan of 1st Brigade was in command. Gen. Morgan spent sixty-three years of his life in the army and died in Quincy, Ill., Sept. 18th, 1896.

The sun shone grandly upon the hedges of bayonets, and flags grew deep and rich in the light, and breasts of dark blue were built into a wall. Aids galloped out from the group around the General, down the line and back to position again. Bugles blew and the stately line was a column. A wing unfolds here, and a wing there. They flapped together as noiselessly as an eagle's. It was an order of march, it was a line of battle. The bugles blew on, and then the field was checkered with squads, like a chess board for a mighty game. They were as true as a die, as exact as a problem in Euclid. There, in equal spaces, between the angles of the square, was formed Barnett's Battery. How it got there nobody could tell. In an instant there was a glitter and a flash. The cavalry were upon them. There was a rustle along the lines, the batteries disappeared, the hedges melted away, the squares were columns, the columns were lines, and away marched the battallions. In all there was no shout, no oath, no loud command.

The General, away yonder upon his horse, moulded and fashioned thousands at will. He could have taken them through Jerusalem's narrow gate, the "needles eye."

The handling of men was a rare art. It was conceded that Major Holmes was the hero of the third brigade in the evolution and movements of a regiment. I have seen a Colonel make three attempts to get his men through a fence gap, two rails wide, and set his men to throwing the rails like a herd of unruly cattle.

The coming of no officer, except a well beloved commander, was so heartily welcomed by the boys, as that gilt-leafed gentlemen with the iron trunk, which gave everything the color of greenbacks. We received two months' pay. The winter had been very severe and it was remarkable how many of the boys overdrew their allowance for clothing. The Government allowed us four dollars a month, and charged us the following prices in the spring of sixty-four: Overcoat $7.50, pants $3.50, blouse $3.12, shoes $1.48, boots $2.87, hat $1.68, cap 54 cents, drawers 95 cents, shirt $1.35, dress coat $6.25, woolen blanket $3.25, rubber blanket $2.55, canteen 44 cents, haversack 48 cents, socks 32 cents.

We must say our clothing was good in quality, as good as we could ask for the price paid, but it was often poorly made. Contractors were foiled in their attempts to defraud the Government in sending out worthless goods. Our trouble was mostly found with the unscrupulous class of men who inspected the goods for the Government

Particularly was this the case with the shoes issued to Sherman's men as we left Savannah for the Carolinas, and the soldiers were outraged by the fraud.

Much of our time was employed in making trinkets to send home. Every company had its craftsman, "a workman that needeth not to be ashamed." Shells of rare

GEO. S. THOMAS, CO. E.

beauty, and exquisite coloring, blue, green, pink and pure pearl, were found in the streams. Look into a boy's knapsack, while we camped at Lee and Gordon's Mills, and you will be quite sure to find a shell in it. Of those queer, broken little shells of former life, the soldier made rings, pins, hearts, arrows, chains, and crosses. When you see the rough tools they used, and note the elegance of form and finish, and the things they made, it would compel one to admit the genius of many a boy who carried a musket. With a flat stone for a polishing tool, he would grind down the shell, and with a knife and file, shape little fancies that would not be out of place in a jeweler's velvet—beautiful souvenirs of battle fields.

This little touch of fine arts gave our camp a pleasant homelike look. We have watched the workmen putting the final touch on a ring, by the light of his inch candle, flaming from a bayonet, as earnestly as if the trinket possessed the charm of Alladdan's lamp, and rubbing it would summon the spirits.

Our camp was on the ground fought over by Rosecrans. Many Union soldiers were buried by the enemy on the field. As we strolled over the field we have seen hands, shriveled and blackened in the sun, looking like some mummy from the Pyramid of Cheops, thrust out of the earth in mute appeal, as a strange memento of the battle. But we thought these sleepers shall spring to resurrection again, in song and story.

Shells were found upon the battle field by relic hunters, and were valuable for the tubing, which was used in making rings. One Sabbath morning we started over the battle-field in search of lumber for the Regimental commissary. On our return a six pound shell was picked up by one of the detail, who, after trying in vain to get the tube out of it, laid it upon a stump and concealing his body, tried to break the shell with a hatchet. It exploded and Jimmy Bond carried home an empty sleeve. Not being injured in the line of duty, he failed for many years in an effort to obtain a pension. He visited Washington City during Corporal Tanner's short reign and was placed upon the pension roll.

The boys delighted in teasing Billy Freeman, the Sergeant Major. Billy was a soldier, every inch of him, having served in the Brittish army seventeen years, and was very particular in requiring promptness in reporting all details. He presisted in saying "horderly," for orderly, and "gobbler" for corporal.

One dark night Billy came down to our quarters, yelling for the "horderly of Company He," and when he had found him, demanded "six men and a gobbler, immediately." The boys began to yell, "horderly," "horderly," while Billy went down the street cursing everybody to "ell."

As he turned out of our Company street he plunged into the Company mess sink up to his belt, and, as it was filled with grease, desiccated vegetables and soup, every boy was out of bed in a minute, listening to his vocabulary of English cusswords.

While we lay in camp at the Mills, many of the boys advertised in the Cincinnati Commercial for young lady correspondents, and scores of them found themselves busy answering letters. This correspondence was generally harmless, and without a single impropriety. For a little amusement, we arranged with the adjutant for answering one of these advertisements. His letters were retained and we kept up the correspondence two or three months, when the scheme was detected by exchange of photographs. How many soldiers thus diverted their minds from the tedium of camp life, and how many acquaintances were formed with profit to the soldier boy.

We stayed so long at Camp Lee and Gordon's Mills that we grew very familiar with everything around us. So familiar that even one of our boys picked out a wife from among the country lasses and they were married in New England style, with apple-jack for the boys, who gave them an old fashioned "down easter" serenade. Quite a number of them were unable to get into camp for roll call in the morning, and took a rest in the guard house. The groom was tied up by the thumbs, by Col. Dan McCook, for marrying the girl contrary to orders. When the war was over he went down to Georgia, hunted up his little southern wife and settled there. Maj. Holmes had his iron gray horse severely kicked on the stifle at McAfee Church, and left it with a native, near Lee and Gordon's Mills. When we were mustered out our adopted son of the new south received an order from the Major to get his horse and ride it through to Ohio. He got the horse, but lost his way, and has not yet arrived. The Major, however, thinks that the recording angel blotted out that item, as the poor boy suffered enough when Col. Dan tied him up for marrying the southern girl.

It commenced snowing at midnight, Saturday the 22nd, and continued until noon the next day. Eleven inches of snow fell. Our company was on picket and we slept without shelter. At daylight, we raised up and saw little mounds like a grave-yard, and as the sleeping soldiers arose, there came to us a vivid picture of the resurrection from the dead. We returned to camp in the morning, in time to take part in the greatest battle of our army service, the battle of "Snow balls." The 52nd and the 86th Ill. were pitted against each other. The fun went on until the whole brigade became involved. Charge after charge was made, one side or the other carrying off as prisoners the officers who led their men. At one time we had several officers of the 86th, while they had our "Own Holmes." A flag of truce was sent in and terms of peace were negotiated. It was a great day of fun. We started one morning in force at ten o'clock, for a reconnoitre to stir up Bragg and let him know we were "doing business at the same old stand." We stopped at Tunnell Hill for the night, meeting only a small cavalry force. Next morning we drove the enemy down towards Mill Creek gap, where we found them buzzing like a hive of bees at morning time. We called at a house by the roadside and while examining the contents of a barrel, brought up from the bottom a new silk rebel flag which had been presented to the 8th Georgia regiment by the ladies of Dalton. On entering the house, we found a captain of that regiment sick, but concealed under the bed. He was home on a sick furlough and had brought the flag with him to have the letters embroidered on it. Col. Clancy sent the flag home after our return to camp.

"Better is a friend that is near than a brother that is far off," so says the old proverb. Our dearest friends seemed to be far off. We thought of our mothers and sisters as our dearest friends and could not bear the thought of having them share with us in the rude usages of camp life. So we were shocked on the morning of the 26th, when we heard we had an assistant surgeon in place of Dr. Rosa, Dr. Mary E. Walker. How she got her commission no one seemed to know. She wrote me that Gen. Thomas commissioned her, and we think that is correct. It seems that she never was carried on the rolls nor do we find her name on the Roster of Ohio soldiers. Possibly, she never was mustered, but she draws a pension from the government as an assistant surgeon.

She was born in Oswego, N. Y., in 1832, and graduated in a medical college in Columbus, O , in 1855. She commenced the practice of medicine in that city the same year, and that may account for her coming to our regiment. She says, "I served as acting assistant surgeon of the 52nd Ohio." She had the rank of 1st Lieutenant and was dressed just like any other officer. The uniform was dark blue and the trousers had a strip of gold lace down the side. She wore curls, so that everybody would know she was a woman. She was thirty-two years of age and had practiced in her profession five years. In form she was slender and rather frail looking in body. The men seemed to hate her, and she did little or nothing for the sick of the regiment. She began to practice in her profession among the citizens in the surrounding country. Every day she would pass out of the picket line, attending the sick. All this time many of the boys believed her to be a spy. One day a messenger came after her from the reserve picket post on the road to Lafayette. A squad of rebel cavalry took her prisoner and she was sent to Richmond, where she was a prisoner in Libby four months. After her exchange she visited the regiment shortly after the battle of Jonesboro.

At the close of the war Congress awarded her a medal of honor. She worked in the Treasurery and Pension departments at Washington, but she was in constant trouble

LIEUT. JAMES H. DONALDSON, CO. E.

and was finally discharged. We believe she was honest and sincere in her views, posing as a reformer, yet the majority of the men in the regiment believed she was out of her place in the army, and have so treated her since the war. She is still living near Oswego, the place of her birth. Her hair is almost white at the age of 68. Her brother left her a farm with a charming old-fashioned house on it, where she has started a training school for wives.

Did you ever go out with a flag of truce? If not, let me give you a little of what I saw one afternoon on picket. A group of horsemen approached our line with a white flag. They were halted, and wheeled about, their backs to the federal lines, their rank demanded, and a messenger dispatched to headquarters, announcing the arrival and asking if the flag would be received and an interview granted. A Yankee officer of equal rank with the bearer of the message was sent out and they each saluted the flag. But what surprises you most, is to see that they shook hands and smiled like old friends. The officers bearing and receiving the message, dismount, move apart and confer. The errand was to pass a lady through our lines to the north.

The little conference over, they mingle on that hand breadth of neutral ground, spend a few minutes in conversation, apparently free and frank, salute each other and wheel away, returning each to his own, while we looked on, leaning upon our muskets.

Flags of truce and the bearing of hostile pickets toward each other always puzzled those who were not in the war. They thought that the two armies had nothing but the deadliest hatred toward each other. And yet nothing can be farther from the truth. Right on the eve of battle we have munched biscuits that our neighbors have tossed us. And two days after the battle of Jonesboro I saw a plug of tobacco in a picket's pocket that showed the print of a rebel's teeth at one end, and a yankee's at the other.

CHAPTER IX.

W E are about to start on the Atlanta Campaign. The 52nd Ohio mustered 519 officers and men, 261 of whom were killed or wounded before Atlanta fell. The regiment served to the end of that campaign in the third brigade, second division, fourteenth army corps, The brigade was commanded by Col. Dan McCook, until he was killed in the assault at Kenesaw Mountain The brigade consisted of 85th, 86th and 125th Illinois, 52nd Ohio, and 22nd Indiana Infantry and Barnett's 2nd Illinois Battery, Company I.

The 86th Illinois was organized at Peoria, Ill., August 27, 1862, Col. Robert S. Moore commanding. The regiment was recruited in Mason, Tazwell, Fulton, Menard, Woodford and Schuylar counties, with an aggregated strength of 959. The regiment mustered out at the close of the war 322 men They were fine looking men, and made a record of which their state is justly proud.

The 86th Illinois was organized at Peoria the same date, August 27th, 1862, Col. David D. Irons commanding. The regiment was recruited in Woodford, Marshall, Peoria, Knox and Tazwell counties, with an aggregated strength of 993 men, and had 468 when mustered out. The regiment made a fine record and the 52nd can refer with pleasure to many acquaintances they formed in three years of army life.

The 125th Illinois was organized at Peoria, September 4th, 1862, Col. Oscar T. Harmon commanding, with an aggregate strength of 933 and mustered out 424 men. They were brave men and true, proudly sustaining the record of our brigade in the Atlanta Campaign.

The 22nd Indiana was organized in 1861, being recruited from the counties of Clark, Scott, Jefferson, Brown, Washington, Floyd, Bartholamew, Jackson and Jennings, Jeff. C. Davis commanding.

The regiment had just returned from a veteran furlough the first of May and Gen. Davis had it assigned to our brigade. Col. Mike Gooding succeeded Davis. Col. Tom Shea lost his right arm at Peach Tree Creek. The regiment lost heavily at Kenesaw and could be depended on always in a fight.

The Second Division was commanded by Gen. Jeff. C. Davis, and the Fourteenth corps by Gen. John M. Palmer. The army of the Cumberland by Gen. George H. Thomas. Grant was now in command of all the Union forces and arranged a concert of action between the east and the west. There was a completeness about the campaigns of 1864, which rendered that year of the conflict an interesting study in modern warfare.

Grant was then about forty years of age. He had dark sandy hair, light blue eyes, a bearded face, a general indifference, but not slouchiness, of figure. He went about unattended, with his head down, and much of the time with his hands in his pockets. But he was the conqueror of Vicksburg and Chattanooga, and commander in chief of more than a million men. With Grant commanding in the east and Sherman in the west, both resolved on victory, believing they would achieve it. Sherman said to Gen. Donaldson, chief commissary at Nashville, "I am going to move on Johnson the day Grant telegraphs me, he is going to move on Bobby Lee, and if you don't have my army supplied and keep it supplied, we'll eat your mules up, sir—eat your mules up.".

W. J. BRADFIELD, CO. C.

Fortunately we were not reduced to such rations, but it well shows his loyalty and spirit.

Gen. Sherman was then in the prime of life, a tall brisk wiry man with dark reddish hair, inclining to baldness, sharp blue eyes, kindly as a rule, but cold and hard as steel sometimes; an aggressive, fighting nose and mouth, considerable of a jaw, and a face a mass of wrinkles. He usually wore only a simple blouse, but always with his proper shoulder straps on, and was noted for his high shirt collar. He impressed you at once as a keen, wide awake man of affairs, with a mind and a will of his own.

Knowing what was needed and resolute to do it, he was the soul of honor, of spotless integrity, a royal friend and a kindly gentleman. As a great companion of Lincoln, Grant and Thomas, his place in history is secure forever. I refer to these great leaders, knowing that you, my comrades of the 52nd, are proud of them, and that we shall not lose sight of them in continuing the history of the regiment.

Gen. Sherman began the Atlanta campaign with 98,797 men and 254 guns. It is true he outnumbered Johnson, who could muster May 1st, 58,000. By the 25th of May reinforcements numbering fully 22,000 were added, but we must consider that Sherman was on the aggressive in the heart of the enemy's country, groping his way over the mountains and through wooded valleys, with at least 20,000 of his army guarding his rear, while Johnson was on the defensive, at home, concentrated, and largely fortified—a big and weighty difference in warfare.

Let me give you some idea of our source of supplies. We could not fight battles without powder, neither could we win them without pork. Bread and bayonets go together. The life nerve of Sherman's army was one line of railroad, running across three states, and three great rivers —and the wonder is that these supplies reached the army at all. From Louisville to Nashville, 185 miles, from Nashville to Chattanooga 155 miles, and from Chattanooga to Atlanta 140 miles, a total of 475 miles. How that railroad was ever kept in repair I cannot tell. It carried the victors and the vanquished. burdens of hope and heavy loads of pain. The wounded and the dead all passed along those tattered railings. Night and day, day and night, forever to and fro move the army legions.

Besides the railway, there was the unbroken column of army wagons, enough of them to make a train two hundred and twenty miles long. Hear the rumbling over that bridge of boats across the Tennessee, as if the long roll were forever beating. These bear the munitions of life without which the munitions of war would be harmless. The mountain achievements of Hannibal and Bonaparte were trifles in comparison.

When Sherman commenced pounding away at Johnson, his nearest supply depot was 153 miles distance, and I do not remember that we were ever short of rations during the entire one hundred and twenty days. As I saw the white canvass of the wagons through clouds of dust, coming and going, I could liken them to a colony of ants, each hastening away with its little white grain of an egg—and these wagons are to supply almost a hundred thousand men, who are marching to victory.

Gen. Palmer concentrated the Fourteenth corps at Ringold on the 3rd of May, while our division advanced to Stone Church, three miles south of Ringold, where we camped on the evening of the 4th. On Saturday May 7th, the campaign opened in earnest, the only fighting of consequence being at the center. Gen. Davis was in the advance with the 52nd Ohio, Maj. Holmes commanding on the skirmish line. Our skirmishers drove the enemy's cavalry steadily until they drew fire from the enemy's guns on Tunnel Hill. Barnett's battery was brought up and McCook's brigade deployed.

The lines again advanced, Maj. Holmes making an attack below the town, for which he was complimented in Davis's report.

Stanley came up on our right, rendering the enemy's position untenable and they retreated toward Mill Creek Gap.

The 52nd Ohio can claim the honor of the first infantry regiment to meet the enemy in that campaign. The 125th Ohio, a splendid fighting regiment, known as the "Opdycke Tigers," the second, as they were selected to open the battle on the next day. We were agreeably surprised to find that no damage had been done to the tunnel or the railroad. As we halted beyond the tunnel we could look into the gorge by which the railroad passed through a straight and well defined range of mountains, presenting sharp faces of rock known as "Rocky Face" or "Buzzard's Glory". Through this defile, Mill Creek flowed toward Dalton, which had been dammed up by the enemy, making a sort of an irregular lake, covering the road a half a mile or more, thus obstructing it. The position was the strongest one, perhaps, between us and Atlanta, and Uncle Billy Sherman had no intention of storming it, yet the next morning we pushed up the face of the hill until part of our line was on the summit.

The fight was kept up all day, the men keeping under cover of rocks and trees and firing at every one that showed a hand above the works. In advancing our line we moved to the right flank. In company with Julius Byers, we were loading and firing when he fell, a ball from the enemy passed through both elbow joints, the shock to the brain killing him instantly.

From the lofty summit there was a magnificent view. The ridge separated the hostile armies. Looking back, as far as the eye could reach, we saw great masses of soldiers in blue; guns were stacked, and men were waiting for orders to move. Some were marching and taking position on the line on the other side. In plain view were the enemy's camps, swarming with men in gray and "butternut". At night we could see the camp fires gleaming and twinkling for miles, showing the position of both armies, and could hear a chaplain distinctly as he preached in the rebel camp below, and joined them in singing the closing hymn, "Am I a soldier of the cross".

A very strange incident occurred on the line during the day. A member of the 125th Ohio was firing, had just raised his rifle to the shoulder and was ready to pull the trigger, when a ball from the enemy entered the muzzle of his gun, causing the rifle to drop from his hands. Had the muzzle of his gun varied a fourth of an inch either way he would have been killed. We were relieved before midnight by one of Harker's regiments.

Morning broke. It was a Scottish morning and the air was dim with mist, but we were ready and eager for the fray. We had put our hands to the burning plowshare and

CORP. JOSEPH M. THOMPSON, CO. E.

here was no thought of turning back. At five we were on our way to Snake Creek Gap, with the 23rd Corps behind us.

The men who shouldered the pen during the war—the correspondents—sneeringly told how fields were won fighting with shovels. The man who successfully starts out on a campaign no more forgets the pick and shovel than he forgets the powder. Sherman never marched without the tools and never halted without entrenching. After the battle of Chickamauga, Gen. Johnson of Mississippi, said to Bragg, "Having beaten the enemy, why didn't you pursue the advantage?" "Well," replied Bragg, "my losses were heavy and my line was pretty long and by the time I could get under motion the yankees would have been ten feet under ground." So we considered the pick ax and shovel as weapons of war.

Thus we moved out that morning, each regiment followed by the shovel brigade. We marched very slowly during the day, but made up the delay by marching all night, resting an hour, about three in the morning. We were getting ready to make coffee when the officers shouted "fall in". We marched up the valley with the inevitable coffee kettle swinging from our bayonets. If the Yankee soldier had been a fellow traveler with Bunyon's Pilgrim, I almost believe that tin kettle of his would be heard tinkling after him to the very threshold of the "gate beautiful".

We learned at daylight that Dalton had been evacuated the night before and Johnson had fallen back to his second base of fortifications at Resaca, from Dalton to Resaca being about 25 or 30 miles. There we are to have a new experience. We came to a halt. The campfires were twinkling in the morning twilight. More than ten thousand men are camped here; valley and hill are tangled in a net work of paths. Everywhere are soldiers sitting beneath trees in the open air, or lying on their blankets. Some are writing, yonder sits one playing a flute, another is drawing the long bow, a group over there are discussing Perrysville or Mission Ridge. Around a box of hard tack and a pile of russet slabs of bacon, with sugar, rice and coffee, are gathered a group of men, tin cup and haversack in hand, waiting for their rations. Within the circle stands the 5th sergeant, the company commissary, who answers the prayer, "Give us this day our daily bread". The distribution goes on, while some boy in his bare feet steps upon somebody's slice of bacon, showing you that the army is a capital place to get rid of your notions, where you can settle your loose joints and fall in line with mother earth and fresh air.

A battle usually comes between two breadths of sleep. Saturday morning came and we awoke to find all astir. Troops were moving. We lay upon a hillside part of the forenoon. General Sherman rode along the line in front of us, accompanied by his staff. A solid shot from a rebel battery passed under the neck of his horse, causing him to stand upon his hind feet, but "Uncle Billy" was master of the situation.

The hardest part of the battle was fought in the afternoon. We were ordered to support our battery and charged up a hill, every man carrying a rail, where in twenty minutes we had a line of works, which were held until Johnson withdrew in the night. Our loss up to this time was 29; three killed or died from wounds at Rocky Face, two killed at Resaca, and 23 wounded. F. M. Carter, of Co. C, was killed early in the afternoon. He was a favorite in his company and a splendid soldier. Capt. Sturgis, of Co. B, was severely wounded, and Jock Harrison of the same company lost his right arm at Rocky Face.

Twice our position was assaulted by the enemy, and we shot away 60 rounds of ammunition to the man, yet we suffered less, perhaps, than any regiment on the line.

The enemy shelled us all night, while our battery fired a shot every half hour, which kept us awake. Soldiers did not fear shells except when they came in swarms. They were great hum-buzzing creatures, that went to the tune of "get out of the way," but the minnie ball, that was a miserable little pellet, that was always to be dreaded, "zip" they came, and with a thud, you were placed "hors de combat."

Our total loss was heavy at Resaca, not so many killed, 680, while 3,375 were wounded. A little dutchman of the 108th Ohio, in our Division, had two fingers shot off, as he went back to the rear he passed Gen. Davis, and holding up his wounded hand, he said, "Sheneral how much pension don't you tink I get? Don't you tink I get two pensions."

During a thunder storm in the evening, a drove of cattle, numbering between two and three thousand, stampeded and three or four hundred of them ran into the rebel lines and were never heard of again. Johnson retreated to Dallas in the night, and the Fourth Corps entered Resaca in the morning.

Our Division was at once dispatched down the valley to Rome. We made seventeen miles the first day, and came upon the enemy five miles from Rome. The 22nd Indiana were in advance, pressing the enemy so closely that many prisoners were taken. The regiment lost eleven killed and thirty-two wounded. Among the wounded were the Colonel, Major and Adjutant. In attempting to cross the river on a flat-boat, the rebels opened on us with three six-pounders, striking the flat, and we thought we were lost. Part of our men jumped into the river and swam to shore. Those who could not swim managed to pole her to the landing. We were among the first to enter the city. The rebel cavalry had just gone out, leaving the town a wreck. What they could not carry away they threw into the street. Books and drugs, with merchandise of all kinds, dumped into the middle of the street in a promiscuous pile. We picked up a copy of Webster's unabridged dictionary and arranged with our company teamster to carry it until we could ship it home. Being scarce of money, he traded it for a plug of tobacco, and my ambition to save it as a souvenir of the war was forever blasted. An immense amount of stores, consisting of rice, sugar, flour and cotton was found, showing us that the enemy had been surprised,

J. P. KENDRICK, CO. B.

CHAPTER X.

THE love for the old flag gushed out unexpectedly like a spring in a desert. Many a Union prisoner has been startled into tears at finding a friendly heart beating close beside him. A few days before we entered Rome, a squad of Union prisoners passed through Rome on their way to Andersonville. They were treated shamefully by the rebel women; pelted with cotton balls and greeted with jeers and taunts. An officer who was among the prisoners, sat down, sick and worn out, with his face in his hands. A lad pulled the officers coat, and catching his breath, boy fashion, said, "are you from New England?" "I was born in Massachusetts," was the reply, "So was my mother," returned the boy. "She was a school marm. She married my father and I'm their boy. How she loves the old flag, so do I." The officer cut a button from his coat and gave it to him for a remembrance. We met that boy, Eddie Ransom, during our stay in Rome, and have wondered many a time what became of him.

The capture of Rome was unexpected to Gen Sherman. When Gen. Davis was detached at Resaca, we had orders to follow Garrard's cavalry down the Oostanaula to the mouth of Armuchee creek, where it was supposed a bridge existed by which Garrard's and Davis' men were to cross and destroy the railroad between Rome and Kingston and then rejoin the main column. Gen. Davis marched 16 miles on the 16th. In the night Garrard passed through his camp enroute for

Resaca, reporting no bridge to be found. Gen. Davis then determined on his own responsibility to advance to Rome and secure the bridge there.

Sherman was moving steadily toward Dallas. Johnson was snugly entrenched behind the Allatoona hills. Sherman marched twenty five miles south to Dallas, leaving the railroad, thus compelling Johnson to retreat to Marietta.

Our Division marched from Rome by the way of Vanwert, to join our corps, the 14th, on the 25th. The battle of New Hope church was fought mainly by Hooker's corps. The church was four miles north east of Dallas. Sherman superintended this battle in person, and I was informed by a comrade of the 79th Pennsylvania, that the General slept the first night by the side of a log, with no covering but a blanket, which one of the boys of that regiment shared with him.

We were temporarily assigned to a place in the line between McPherson and Joe Hooker. The next day an assault was made on our immediate right, which was repulsed with heavy loss to the enemy. During the lull in the fight, a group of officers were standing in our rear, among whom were Generals Sherman, Logan, McPherson, Burry, chief of artillery, and Colonel Taylor. A minnie ball passed through Logan's coat sleeve, breaking the skin and struck Col. Taylor square in the breast. Luckily he had in his pocket a famous memorandum book in which he noted the day's events. It saved his life, but the ball passed through the book to the ribs, disabling him for the rest of the campaign. The enemy's sharp shooters got range of the only spring near us, and many a boy lost his life in running the gauntlet. Tommy Taylor, Co. E., started for the spring in spite of the remonstrances of his friends, sinking his canteen in the water, when tick—a rifle ball struck it at an angle and bounded away. He thought it a chance shot, a piece of lead without any malice, so again he bent to get the water. Ping a second bullet cut the cord of his canteen, and he said to himself, "sharp shooter," and made for tall timber, "saved by the skin of his teeth." When the notion that somebody is making a target of you, creeps with its chilly feet slowly up your back, you are ready to shrink into yourself, though you may not be quite ready to own it.

On the evening of the 24th a teriffic rain storm came up and the lightning ran along the bayonets of the guns of the First Ohio. They had just taken their hands away, when the lightning seemed to play upon the steel. The whole regiment was severely shocked, yet no lives were lost.

May 29th our division relieved part of Scofield's corps, and the next day we were relieved and marched eight miles, joining our old command under Palmer, having been away just fifteen days. Johnson withdrew from the front and we moved to the railroad near Big Shanty, in sight of the famous Kenesaw mountain.

Thus in one month we had fought our way over rugged hills and mountains, one hundred miles. The sound of musketry and roar of artillery could be heard almost every day. We being on the aggressive our loss was greater than Johnson's, aggregating over nine thousand, theirs was about one thousand less. Two divisions of the 17th corps, under Frank P. Blair, came up the 8th of June. The same had been home on veteran furlough. The reinforcement made good our losses from battle and sickness.

Big Shanty had been made famous by the bold feat of the Andrew's raiders, capturing an engine they started for Chattanooga. Of all the adventures of the war none was more daring. They were caught and most of them were hung. We called them raiders, but the rebels called them spies, and as spies they were hung.

It is said there is nothing in a name, with them it was all in the name. The same engine is one of the curiosities of the war and was a marvel for sight-seers at the World's Fair at Chicago.

We rested at Ackworth a few days, washing our clothes and writing letters. Sunday came, and as our Chaplain scarcely ever had services while on that campaign, we started to find some place where we might worship with the tried and true of the army of the Lord.

After blundering through camp we came upon the 43rd Ohio. The regiment was known as the "Marten box" regiment, as every company in the regiment in the spring time when in camp, erected poles with boxes on the top of them, and there the marten's chatterd every morning and were fed on army rations. The services were just opening. Chaplain Boute had resigned and a friend of Col. Wager Swayne, R. L. Chittenden, had been appointed in his stead. This was his first sermon. He was a young man, neatly dressed, making us think of home and the days of "auld lang syne." The Colonel was an interested listener. As the services began, just in the rear of the audience a kettle was boiling over a fire, where a soldier upon his knees beside it was apparently worshiping the hardware. But he was no idolater, for a closer look discovered him fishing in the kettle with something like a fork. The Chaplain's text was John the Baptist's reply to the question of the soldiers, "what shall we do?" and the answer, "do violence to no man, neither accuse any falsely, and be content with your wages." No matter for the rumbling of the passing trains and the noise of the camp, he kept right on, clear, earnest and sensible, but the text was unfortunate. The Chaplain was ignorant concerning the situation. The boys had not been paid for six months, and they were indignant at the godly man's boldness in chiding them tor the curses they had heaped on "Uncle Sam" for a lack of promptness in not sending them their hard earned wages. They were mad and felt like whooping him out of camp, and yet I could not help feeling a profound respect for the man and the little group of worshipers at his feet.

We began to close in and around the enemy's position, which embraced three steep ranges of hills, known as Kenesaw Pine mountain and Lost mountain. In a day or two the railroad was repaired up to the skirmish line. One day an engine was detached from a train, and ran into the gorge between Little and Big Kenesaw, to a water tank within range of the rebel guns, in order to find the location of the batteries. The run was made by the engineer, the tank open, the tender filled, and returned answering the peal of the enemy's guns by the scream of the whistle, while the shouts and cheers of our men rang over mountain and down the valley. Gen. Sherman was so well pleased with the daring of the engineer, that he grasped his hand and thanked him for his bravery, offering to pay him, but the hero refused to take the money, saying, "I only did my duty and am amply repaid in your hearty approval." Bishop Taylor often referred to this incident, as an illustration of the relation of duty to reward.

The rain continued to pour and make our movements very slow, entrenching as we went and building "corduroy" for our supply trains. You would be interested in the movement of a whole division in the night—flanking the Jonnies it was called—sometimes a mile, sometimes more, I could never tire of telling you how iron-like the men got to be, but like the best machinery ever made, the continued wear and exposure told on the toughest constitution and one by one they began to drop out, and the regiment nearly 1100 strong, now stacks 478 guns. It is screened like grain and the sturdiest manhood only remain. By June 14th the

JULIUS B. WORK, CO. G.

rain slackened a little and we occupied a continuous line of ten miles, conforming to the irregular position of the enemy. During the day we noticed a group of rebel officers, belonging to a battery, were hurrying to and fro on the top of the mountain; finally they gathered with an officer and his staff, who were inspecting our dinner by the aid of a field glass.

A Prussian officer, who was in command of an Indiana battery, known as "Leather breeches," ordered his men to "shust tickle dem fellows." The second shot struck rebel general Polk in the breast and cut him in two. Gen. Polk was bishop of the Episcopalean diocese of Mississippi at the breaking out of the war, and thus sacrificed life and all for the south.

Our signal officer, having obtained the key to the rebel signals, read the signal from Pine Mountain to Marietta, saying, "Send an ambulance for Gen. Polk's body," and this report was confirmed later in the day by prisoners who had been captured.

The signal corps was indispensible in our movements. Dispatches were thus sent from hill top to hill top, thus keeping up communication with all parts of the field. Had you been with us on picket at night, you might have seen on the highest eminence, a light somewhat larger than the planet Venus at the full, swinging after a mad fashion, and near it another light. But after you had watched it for awhile you would have discovered that there was method in that madness, every motion of that light meant something. You watch it and it describes a quadrant, makes a semi-circle, stops, rises, sweeps left, rounds out an orbit and strikes off at a tangent. The officer of the signal corps is talking to somebody. In the daytime the officer gesticulates with flags instead of the light, and so the talk goes on around the sky.

It rained again for a week and the weather had a wonderful effect on the troops, especially in the woods where all is blind and uncertain. An order came to "fall in" and get your whiskey, known as "commissary whiskey." One of the boys, after he had drank his ration, which was a gill, said that he could smell the boy's feet that had plowed the corn out of which it had been made. The medical director had drugged it with quinine and other "microbe killers." Rations of whiskey were only issued five times during our three years of army life, and yet we never suffered malaria or fever during our enlistment.

Here Henry Webber, of Co. I, was killed by a premature bursting of one of our own shells, while the next shot from the rebel guns on the mountain struck a boy, lying in his tent asleep, and cut him in two. He belonged to the 85th Illinois.

Next day it cleared up and the sun came out. We could see where we were. Stanley's and Wood's Divisions made a successful charge on our right, taking a hill which the enemy tried to retake three times without success. It was here that the 15th and 97th Ohio suffered the greatest loss of the campaign.

Sitting the next morning just over our line of breastworks, under a clump of bushes, writing our weekly message home, unmolested, except an occasional shot from the mountain, there was a flash, a long, rushing, shivering cry and a shell strikes in the mud embankment, exploding and covering us with earth. We beat a hasty retreat, landing in the ditch among the boys. Our battery charged a Rodman twelve-pounder. It speaks and down comes a carriage of an angry gun for kindling wood and we throw up our hats, and at it the batteries went. A shell that does its duty has thunder and a cloud at both ends of its flight.

On the 25th of June we were resting one mile to the rear of the front line, facing Little Kenesaw. The 26th was Sunday and seemed to be the quietest day we enjoyed since we left Rome. Gen. Logan passed along in the afternoon. Among the men who composed his staff was Captain Gordon Loffland, of Cambridge, O., an old friend and schoolmate. He dismounted and we chatted away about home and friends and bidding me good bye, said, "Old boy, this may be the last time we may meet, for tomorrow morning your division is to make a desperate charge on Little Kenesaw. If successful, it will doubtless be the destruction of Johnson's army. Good bye, and may you come out all right." Col. Dan McCook had been a law partner of Gen. Sherman and had been selected to lead the charge in the center. As the Captain rode away, he turned and said, "Let me hear from you when it is over." I do not think there was a trace of anxiety as I sat down and wrote to friends at home, without a hint of the coming morrow. It was not a question of battle lost or won, of victory or defeat, but something alone and beyond them all. Night came on and we sat down with the boys, who with us had followed the old flag almost two years, who on the coming morn were to go where sheets of flame would baptize them and where plunging shot would thin their ranks.

There was such a beautiful sunset that evening. The trees and woods seemed touched and set on fire. I had thought of the burning bush, but it had come back to me as one of the loveliest pictures of memory. Jest and laughter was heard from the groups gathered here and there to while away the time, while nothing seemed to disturb the steady stroke of an easy-going heart.

CHAPTER XI.

BATTLE OF KENESAW MOUNTAIN.

WE were up at four the next morning with orders to move at six, without knapsacks, but with forty rounds in our cartridge boxes. Thus, before breakfast every boy knew of the day's work before him. The hush of the coming storm was in the air. As I opened that old volume my mother gave me when I left home, I read, "A thousand shall fall at thy side and ten thousand at thy right hand, but it shall not come nigh thee," and commending my life to God, felt an inspiration that followed me throughout the whole day.

When soldiers get ready for battle they generally go like men on business. The old blouse is good enough, the old hat will answer. You may notice they may look to their guns a little more critically; they tighten up their belts a little and are ready. Officers seldom wore their finery in the field. The torn bars, the clipped eagle, the dim star will do, but it is not always so. I have known a soldier to make a most careful toilet on the morning of battle. Sergeant Michie, of Co. H, always put on his best uniform, as if he were going home. Perhaps the chance of such a thing may have drifted into his mind. At other times I have been surprised at what men were thinking about who are going into battle. Gen. Grant, at Orchard Knob, was a quiet gentleman in a snuff-colored coat, while Gen. Jimmy D. Morgan was a twin brother to his orderly. He went into battle in a shocking hat, while there was a glitter of buttons and stars wherever Phil. Sheridan went, and that was in the thickest of the fight. "I want my men to know where I am" he said with a smile. Nothing so inspires the rank and file as faith in their leaders, and no men in that campaign had any better than we had—a McCook, Davis, Thomas and Sherman. Faith in such men, tones men up and makes them braver and nobler every time they are tried. This was preeminently true of our own brave Col. Dan. McCook, who formed our brigade in line that morning. We had heard his clear, shrill voice many a time as he led us from the Ohio to that mountain base. When duty, hardship and danger came in a cluster, he plucked it with a ready grasp, saying, "come boys," and not "go."

At 8 o'clock we moved rapidly to position in rear of our main works. A general attack all along the lines had been ordered, as a diversion in favor of the main assault. The second brigade of our division, Col. John G. Mitchell commanding, was on our right. Our brigade was formed in column of regiments in the following order, 85th Illinois, Col. C. J. Dilworth, deployed as skirmishers; 125th Illinois, Col. O. F. Harmon; 86th Illinois, Lieut. Col. A. L. Fahnestock; 22nd Indiana, Capt. W. H. Snodgrass; 52nd Ohio, Lieut. Col. C. W. Clancy.

As they formed in line, the sun shining clear upon them, the words of Heber's sweet old song came to me in war's bold autograph, and

"You see them on their winding way,
About their ranks the sunbeams play."

Five regiments, not quite 1,800 men. Five pairs of flags, that had rose and fell on the surges of battle, were carried in the center of each battallion. The dyes of the dyer were dim, but the death of those who fell in their defense had made the tints sublime. Those old flags were nothing but silk, yet they had gone up the ladder of meaning, like the angels in the vision of the patriarch. They had become col-

JEHU PECK, CO. D.

ors. Hardee's corps was in our front and left, Hood's corps to our right. The rebel line was almost in the shape of a fishhook, on what is now known as Cheatham's Hill or the Dead Angle. The charge was made on Cheatham's division, composed of Vaughn's, Maney's and Strahl's brigades. We were to strike the circular bend of the works or the lower end of the fish hook.

That beautiful morning was half gone when we were told that all things were ready. The hostile army grimly waited for our coming, as slowly we marched into the jaws of death. Just as the batteries ceased firing, we dressed our lines into column, and Col. Dan. McCook, standing in front of the brigade, repeated from McCauley's poem in Horatius the words:

"Then out spoke bold Horatius, the captain of the gate,
To all men of the earth cometh soon or late.
But how can man die nobler, when facing fearful odds,
For the ashes of his fathers, and the temple of his Gods."

It was fifty paces from McCook's to Morgan's line. We moved promptly on signal, going at quick time, then double-quick, on coming to the creek, which was marshy and sluggish, our lines was somewhat broken.

Firing began immediately. From the crest both musketry and artillery, but we pushed on capturing the line of rifle pits, taking the men prisoners. The batteries opened right and left, as we pushed on up the hill. It is dreadful to think about. Grape and canister, shot and shell sowed the ground with rugged iron and garnished it with the dead. The first to fall was Sergeant John T. Fowler, of Co. B. As he fell, his tongue protruded from his mouth, caused by a contraction of the muscles of the throat. I longed to take him in my arms and minister to his sufferings, but we were to push the battle. The race of flags grew every moment more terrible. Four color-bearers were either killed or wounded. Linley H. Street, a brave boy, beloved by his comrades, fell, pierced to death. Sergeant Wm. J. Bradfield snatches the flag and is wounded in the strong right arm as he leads the charging column. Poor boy, he goes back to Nashville to die with the dread gangrene. David U. Mc-Cullough of Co. E, seizes the old banner and is wounded in the shoulder. Thus three of our color-bearers are shot down. The line wavers like a great billow and up comes the banner again. Now it is in the hands of James Lynne of Co. C. He loses an arm and on we go. Sheets of flame baptize us. Plunging shot tear away comrades on left and right. It is no longer shoulder to shoulder, it is God for us all. We are facing the steady fire of two thousand infanty, pouring down upon our heads as if it were the old historic curse from heaven. We wrestled with the mountain, but our brave men are climbing steadily on — upward still. Things are growing desperate. The enemy began to throw stones upon our heads. They light the fuse and throw hand grenades in our faces. One of these struck James Sheets, of Co. E, tearing away all the flesh from his cheek.

They shout down upon us "Chickamauga." Our brave Dan McCook was in the lead, when our front line had reached the fortifications, only to find a barrier which was calculated to make a weak man falter and a brave man think. The works were fringed with pikes, sharpened pins driven into logs, standing like a hay rack, pointing toward your face. Four lines of these stood one behind the other, so arranged that they overlapped each other. In a moment the front line grasped the barrier of pikes, and carried them endways, thus opening the way to the line of earth works.

Our brave Colonel urging his men on, was struck as he said, "Come on boys, the day is won," as he reached the earth work. He was shot about four inches below the collar bone, in the right breast, falling outside of the fortifications.

After the fall of Col. McCook, the voice of Captain Charles Fellows of McCook's staff was heard, but his half finished, "come on boys—we'll take"—was cut short, and brave Charley fell dead only a few feet from the ditch.

Regiment after regiment breasted the storm as we came upon the mountain, until all four of the regiments in front of our line had tried and failed, and when we reached the works, we were in the front line. Several colors were planted in the loose earth at the foot of the ditch. We learned from a member of the 1st Tennessee Infantry, that Capt. Beasley of that regiment lost his life while attempting to grasp the colors of the 52nd Ohio. Our regiment preserved a fair allignment to the last, and was undoubtedly assisted in the final stand by many members of other regiments. No braver and better behaved men ever attempted to storm an impregnable fortress than the Illinois and Indiana boys who were slaughtered in that terrible assault.

Col. Harmon, of the 125th, took command. He gave the command "Forward" and fell into the arms of his men, pierced throught the heart. Deadly volleys mowed us down. The ground was strewn with the dead and dying. The living crouched behind the dead comrades. Col. Dilworth of the 85th Ill., was now the ranking officer, and no sooner in command than he was wounded, and the command was assumed by Lieut. Col. J. W. Langhley, of 125th Ill.

The order had been given to fall back twenty paces and thus straighten our lines which had swung to the right and rear, owing to the galling fire from the lower depression of the enemy's line in that direction. When the order was given to re-form our lines we had lain down right under the enemy's works, and everyone of us would have been killed or captured, had it not been that the line formed twenty-five yards below us with the advantage of the depression of the slope. They, by firing over our heads, soon had control of the line in our immediate front. Probably one-half of our regiment that were unharmed, lay within twelve feet of the earth works and not in a position to load and fire. One by one our men crawled back to the new line below while many of us, with the dead and seriously wounded, lay near the works. Three of my comrades were struck just as our men lay down. Joseph Hanlon lay dead on my right. Isaac Winters, who was shot in the temple, but living, lay within my reach on the left. Frank Grace of Co. D, lay dead just below me, and Joseph E. Watkins of the 22nd Indiana Regiment, rose to start for the line below, when he fell dead across my feet, as I lay near a chestnut stump, within ten feet of the earth works. Col. Clancy was on my left, and in an opportune moment, he started for the line below, catching his foot in the belt of a sword, plunged into our line below, taking the sword with him. It proved to be Capt. S. M. Neighbor's, he, having been seriously wounded a short time before, stripped off his sword and belt and staggered to the rear.

While lying here with a dead soldier across my feet, who could describe the sensations of the forty minutes that passed. To run the gauntlet might be death, to lie there, a movement of the body would draw the fire of the enemy on the "Dead Angle" to our right. The comrade shot in the temple sat up and began to talk in delirium, which attracted the enemy. He plead for water. I pushed my canteen toward him and he reached out but failed to get it.

Sergeant John W. Baltzly, of Co. D, was lying within the ditch and was asked to come over the works. He hesitated, but finding they could get range of his position from the right, the sergeant, red-headed and hatless, went over to spend six months in Andersonville.

Lying to my right and near the breast works, was Newton H. Bostwick, of Co. I, a mere lad of seventeen years.

He wore a cockade hat and white acorn, the badge of our division. Bostwick had been severely wounded in the shoulder, and was ordered to come over the works, which he attempted to do, to save his life. The Sergeant Major of the 1st Tennessee reached over the head log to help the boy. A bullet from our line below missed the rebel and buried it-self in the neck of the already wounded boy. The officer pulled him over the works and sent him to the rear, visiting him after the battle was over. He did not permit him to be sent south until he began to recover, and later in the war furnished him with some delicacies at Macon, Georgia. The brave, boyish soldier was filled with gratitude and giving his name and the address of his parents to the officer, they parted. Young Bostwick was finally exchanged November 24, 1864, and lives in Chardon, Ohio, a leading attorney of Geauga county. In 1880 he wrote the following letter to the Nashville American:

"To the Sergeant Major of the Rock City Guards, C. S. A., or any other Confederate soldier who was at the battle of Kenesaw Mountain, June 27, 1864, Nashville, Tenn.

CHARDON, O., March 13, 1880.

DEAR SIR:—I should like to know something of you. You treated me well while I was a prisoner with you on the field that day (June 27) and I have ever since felt a friendly feeling toward you. I am the boy with the cocked hat and white acorn, who fell inside your works that warm morning in June. You fought like the devil and made a hot place for us to come through, but it always seemed to me that if we could have held out a little longer the fortunes of the day might have changed. Please write to me, I want to know what has become of you boys, and oblige,

N. H. BOSTWICK

The letter was turned over to James A. Jennings, of the 1st Tennessee, who replied as follows:

—121—

MR. N. H. BOSTWICK.

DEAR SIR:—Your interesting favor of the 13th inst. was received today. We right well remember the 27th of June, 1864. I was Sergeant Major and well remember the boy with the cocked hat and acorn—how you were shot through the neck as your men shot at me, and that you was a brave boy. I lost your address. I was captured in Hood's last fight and remained a prisoner until the cruel war was over. We lost but few men at Kenesaw, as we were well fortified. The slaughter on your side was terrible. We were almost out of ammunition, I think if you had put another fresh line in you would have got us, but we had orders to hold that place, and you know what kind of boys we were. Out of 150 Rock City Guards only about 50 are left. They were all brave and did their duty. I think I can say the same for the 52nd Ohio. We would be glad if you could pay us a visit. We will make it pleasant for you. The war is over and we must be the best of friends. In union there is strength. Yours truly,

JAMES A. JENNINGS.

We took our chance for the line below and landed safely. A portion of the new line kept up the firing. The remainder, lying on their faces, working with bayonet and tin cup, managed to throw up a light breastwork, sufficient to protect their prostrate bodies. This work was accomplished while under a severe fire from our right in the angle of the enemy's works. The distance in the charge was made in about forty minutes, but it was two o'clock when we had sufficient protection to feel safe.

Our loss in the 52nd was 34 killed and 102 wounded and three prisoners, total 139. The loss in the brigade was 419. The other four regiments, in the aggregate, losing 280 men; the 52nd, 139, almost one-third of the total loss. Of those who fell, 34 were killed, 11 died of wounds received in the charge.

Our gallant Colonel was missed, so young—not yet twenty-nine, so courteous, so modest, so brave. With the frankness and simplicity of a boy, he united the dash of a Marion and the wisdom of a veteran. How he led us, like the tenth wave of the sea, right into that storm of splintery fire and shotted shell. He fell, but lived long enough to be taken to his home in Steubenville, O., where he died, July 17th, and was buried in Spring Grove cemetery in Cincinnati, beside his father and four brothers, who gave their lives for the old flag.

On the evening of his death his brother, Col. George W. McCook, then colonel of the 157th O. N. G., on duty at Ft. Delaware, while standing before his regiment on dress parade, received a telegram, opened it, and with tears streaming down his face, said to the adjutant, "Take the regiment to their quarters," and wept aloud for a brother he loved so well.

On the 16th of July, the day before our beloved Colonel's death, Gen. Sherman received a commission from Secretary Stanton, for the death-stricken hero, as Brigadier General. When the message was read to him, on his bed of suffering, he said, "The promotion is too late now, return my compliments, saying 'I decline the honor'," and every man in the brigade honored his refusal of that which he had earned more than a year before.

I would love to speak personally of every man in the regiment, for every one of them did their duty. No troops in the late war bore themselves with greater honor than they. Gen. Davis sent us word that nothing could be done until nightfall, in getting tools to fortify, as our men would be shot down in crossing the valley of Noyes creek. But we were not to be baffled. One-half of the men worked while the rest hugged the ground and shot at every Johnny reb, who dared show his head.

The whole brigade was massed in two lines. One line in the front being one hundred and one feet from the head log of Johnson's works. After dark came on the dead and wounded close to our line were collected. Some of the wounded succeeded in rolling down to us. This was the case with Capt. Joseph Majors, of the 86th, who was struck with a rock during the charge and came to consciousness in the night, and instead of walking came rolling into our lines.

Night came, we were glad of it. Our canteens were empty, so were our cartridge boxes The enemy fired a volley of musketry, which no doubt was to prevent our working on the fortifications. An hour after dark they rolled cotton balls in turpentine and threw them over, setting the dry twigs and leaves on fire, burning and charring our dead. The cries of some, who were wounded and not dead, was horrifying to us.

JOHN MOORE, CO. F.

CHAPTER XII.

KENESAW EVACUATION, BATTLE OF PEACH TREE CREEK
AND JONESBORO.

THE 28th found us with our armor on and worthy and well qualified to hold what advantage we had secured the day before. They opened on us with their batteries, but were silenced by our guns in the rear.

During supper, a command from the other side was heard, clear and distinct, "make ready, take aim, fire!" over came stones and clubs, pick handles and frying pans, and woe be to the man who was unprotected. Many on our line were struck and disabled. Capt. Mansfield was crippled for life. Serg. Major, Wm. Freeman was struck with a pick handle, went to the hospital and never returned for duty.

Wednesday morning a truce lasting from 9 a. m. to 4 p. m. was arranged to bury the dead. Unarmed guards, detailed from each side, were stationed in two lines, facing outward, to prevent the passing of other than the burial party, which worked between. A general exchange of news papers, coffee and tobacco while a jolly good feeling abounded everywhere. Our dead had lain upon the ground forty hours and the smell was terrible. Thirty-seven of our brigade were buried in the four hours in which we worked. It was my good fortune to be on the detail and to be able to identify all who belonged to the 52nd Ohio. We dug the graves, right where they lay, covering them over and marking the spot with the name and regiment. Our men sat upon the head logs and crowds of armed men from the commands near by thronged our works. The rebel line was crowned with sightseers of high and low rank. Generals from both sides circulated freely between the lines, although this was in direct violation of the terms of the truce. Hindman, Cheatham and Maney were prominent. I was particularly interested in Pat Cleburne, who afterwards lost his life at Franklin. He was tall, with a genial face and a good fighter, as we had a chance to know. We sat down and chatted with the detail and enjoyed ourselves like friends. A challenge came from a rebel who wanted to wrestle with any yank in the crowd. It was accepted by one of our boys, a recruit. He threw the Johnny, amid the shouts of our boys. The signal gun was fired and we were pecking away at each other in five minutes.

"Necessity is the mother of invention." A comrade of the 125th Illinois invented a life preserver and at the same time a rebel killer. A small piece of looking glass, two and a half inches square, framed with zinc, with a wire stem by which it was attached to the stock of our Springfield rifles, so arranged that we could lie down in the trench, the rifle resting on the breast works, pointing toward the rebel head-log, that you could look through the sights and with your hammer pulled back, pick off a rebel without exposing the body. Hundreds of these were made and used to the astonishment of the men opposite to us. A large chestnut tree, hollow at the lower side, was used as a fortress, from which our men watched through the glass for a shot. An orderly came over one morning from Gen. Davis's headquarters, anxious to try the new invention. He entered the hollow tree, waiting for an opportunity. Becoming excited, he exposed the side of his head, when a sharp shooter in the "Angle" put a bullet hole through his ear and the poor boy went down the hill like an army in full retreat.

A daring feat was performed in broad daylight, on the afternoon of the 30th. A well dressed man in federal uniform, new and clean, a mess pan in one hand, a small bucket steaming with hot coffee in the other, when the outpost where three comrades were stationed half way between our works and the enemy's and were protected by the double trunk of a large tree, where they watched the movement of the men in the rebel trenches, was reached the stranger passed to one side and dropping his pan and coffee, with several bounds disappeared over the enemy's parapet. No one had time to realize that he was a spy—so rapidly did he complete his perilous journey. ''The Memphis Appeal,'' then published in Atlanta, the next morning, published an account or the daring feat. The spy, no doubt, furnished the information that McCook's brigade had such close proximity to Cheatham's line that they had already tunneled under his breast works, and that they had experimented as to the fact reported, by placing a drum in the trench occupied by their men, by laying marbles on a drumhead, they distinctly noticed the rattle of the marbles at every stroke of the pick, made by the sappers and miners in the tunnel beneath. That night they opened on us with a terrible musketry fire, which lasted an hour or more.

We were in close quarters almost six days. During this time we shot away probably two hundred rounds of ammunition to the man. When we could not see a Johnny to shoot at we fired away at the flag staff the rebels put up on their breast works. Several times it was shot off, and the emblem of treason fell to the ground. Wm. F. Carson, of Co. B, was killed the morning of the 22nd of July. Poor Will was absent minded, he raised his head above the head log and was killed. Thirty-four of the regiment were killed or wounded on the line in the six days after the charge. The First, Fourth, Sixth, Ninth, Nineteenth and Twenty-seventh Tennessee regiments, veterans on the rebel side, were in the works opposite to us. They had the best protection that coula be constructed, while our brigade confronted them in their works, which were seven feet high and twelve feet thick. Practically no part of our assaulting column was captured and one brigade lay within a stone's throw of the works until the enemy retreated. About one o'clock, Sunday morning, a voice from the rebel works shouted, "Don't shoot down there, they are done gone from here." We asked him to come over and a detail to reconnoiter was made. They were gone from our front. The 23rd Corps cautiously advanced, while we lay in our works until morning.

It was Sunday. At daybreak our band played "Old Hundred," while we sang "Praise God from whom all blessings flow." It was joy to our boys as we had scarcely looked up for six days from our dangerous position. Marietta was ours, and our forces were pushing Johnson toward Atlanta.

We rested a few days at the Chattahoochie. Atlanta was only eight miles distant, almost in hearing of Sherman's drum beat As we crossed the river, we asked an old slave tottering with age, how long he had been there. He said, "Oh massa, I'se been heah ever since I was born, ever since dis river was a little bit of a stream."

Johnson was relieved and Hood was now in command, and the people would tell us that_ Sherman would have to fight now, there would be no more driving the Southern army "end ways."

The iron heart of Sherman's column began to beat as his batteries thundered at the gates of Atlanta. Up to July 19th, there had been no battle since we left Kenesaw, only skirmishing and dashes of cavalry and soundings of the lines on our front.

Early in the morning of the 19th, we pushed our skirmishers across Peach Tree Creek, crossing on a log twenty-eight feet from bank to bank. The water was about eight feet deep and could not be forded. While we were laughing at an unlucky fellow in Co. H, who fell from the foot-log, the rebels opened fire on us from their skirmish line, As we reached the top of the hill, the enemy poured a galling fire on our right flank, and turned our left by a heavy reinforcement. The 98th Ohio had crossed above us, and came to our rescue, the enemy retreating into a dense pine thicket. The left wing of our regiment, with Col. Clancy, was deployed in front and pushed down into the pines and lay down. The regiment worked like beavers completing a barricade of rails, behind which they lay. The advance sentinels came rushing back, shouting, ''They are charging in front, four lines deep, with fixed bayonets.'' We must get out to let our men in the works open fire. " 'Twas madness to defer." It was run the gauntlet or be taken to Andersonville prison, or death. They were upon us. The Colonel with thirteen men went to prison, the rest filed to the right, down a small ravine, and started for liberty or death. It was the devil's own corner. We were but half way from the starting point to the brow of the hill when the enemy poured a deadly volley into our ranks. Here twenty-nine of the one hundred and fifty-four fell, dead or wounded, knelt at the shrine were those that were dead, and never rose from worshiping. Over the works we went, to find the whole line with fixed bayonets, expecting a hand to hand conflict.

Such firing as those comrades did do, as they cheered those who had escaped death. The rebel line falters—it stopped— it fled. Our loss was heavy, twenty-one killed and forty-seven wounded. Five of Co. E lost their lives. Lieut. James H. Donaldson,Samuel M. Hanlin,Eli Gordon, Elias Dimmit, dead, and John F. Rightly, mortally wounded. Lieut. Donaldson had drawn a new patent leather haversack that morning, remarking as he put it on, "I will be a shining mark for the Johnnies." He was shot through the haversack. Hanlon was shot through the thigh, severing an artery. Taking off his suspenders, he tied a knot in one of them, placing the knot over the artery, stopped the flow of blood. When dark came, we crawled to where he lay and found him dying from exhaustion. Many strange things occurred that morning. Elias Dimmit, of our company, said to me, "I will be killed today, send my Bible and pictures to mother." He fell in the recall of our skirmishers, shot through the knapsack, through eight folds of a rubber blanket and twenty-nine leaves of writing paper, out through his heart.

It was a hand-to-hand conflict on the right of the regiment. Among those who fell, there was none braver than Captain Schneider. His home was in Brooklyn Village, now a part of Cleveland. At the time of his death he was twenty-eight and engaged to an excellent young lady of Cleveland. He received a letter from her the evening before the battle, urging him to resign and come home, as she had fears he would be killed in the next battle. The Captain said to Major Holmes, "I have a dread presentiment of it myself, but my country is in peril. If I fall,

"Let me fall in the van
Of the conquering host."

The Captain had been jealous over Major Holmes's promotion. It had wounded him. He had treated the Major with suspicion, but the evening before the battle he freely opened his heart to him, and said, "I am your friend and want to confess that my suspicions were all unfounded. I am your truest friend." When he was found his revolver was in his hand with one barrell empty. A rebel Major lay dead within a few feet of him. The hole in the Major's head was made by a 32 calibre, the same as the Captain's revolver, and the Major's bullet had struck the Captain in the temple. Both were dead.

Frank Miser, of Co. G, fell, mortally wounded. He was left on the battle field for a few hours, when his comrades returned he was dead. In his hand was a discharge paper from a hospital in Cincinnati, on the back of it was written these words, with a pencil, "Dear father and mother, I am mortally wounded. I die like a soldier, and hope to meet you all in heaven."   B. F. MISER.

On the eve of the battle, we have heard such talk as this, "I expect to be in the hottest place in the field tomorrow, but do you know the bullet is not run that will kill me," and the brave boy dropped off into a child-like sleep, while I lay awake and was troubled. A little after four the next afternoon, a bursting shell carried away the "pound of flesh" that Shylock craved, and again he fell asleep, only to awake at the call of God's trumpet.

The next morning we went to the hospital to see how our boys were getting along It was a beautiful ridge ; tall, slim oaks sprinkle it, and beneath them stand the tents of the field hospital. Within them lie the men, who charged the hill yesterday, marred with wounds and wasted with pain, parched with fever, wearily turning, wearily waiting to take up the blessed march. They are to go North. It is Chattanooga, it is Nashville, it is home and it is heaven, but they are hopeful and heartful for they will go "bye and bye." We returned to the hillside. Near our lines a grave is being dug. Four boys in their brown blankets, four labels, with four names on four still breasts. The four bodies were lifted and borne away to that wide open grave on the hillside and one after another lowered into the grave. As we looked for the last time into their faces, we silently said, "Lord, if thou had'st been here my brother had not died," and then we prayed a soldier's prayer for the flag, and those that bear it, and for the four mothers, yonder at home, whose hearts will yearn, but to see them no more. After filling the grave and setting up the tablet, on which was written the names, Lieut. James H. Donaldson, Samuel M. Hanlon, Eli Gordon and Elias Dimmit, we turned away thinking, "So dies in human hearts the thought of death," for a bird in a tree near by sang as if nothing had happened, and the sun shone on as if there were no clouds in the world save those that float in the heavens.

Hood furiously assaulted our left on the 22nd, where the brave McPherson fell with many of his brave men, and failing to break our lines, withdrew within his fortifications. As we were on the front line, the regiment suffered more or less every day. One morning Lieut. Adam Knecht and six men of Co. A were wounded and one killed. Courtman, Armstrong and Flynn, of Co. H, and Otho Linton, of Co. E, were also killed. One morning a message came by "grape vine" that we were ordered to Ohio to enforce the draft. The boys began to discuss the probability of a winter campaign among the rebels of the North. Our first move was to be against Fort Fizzle in Holmes county, and then with banners flying, we were to put down the rebellion at Hoskinsville in Noble county. But Burns reminded us that "The best laid schemes o' mice and men, gang aft 'agley". So we kept pegging away at Hood's army, with faith in God and old Billy Sherman, knowing that the end was nigh.

Sunday evening came. It was sultry and all was quiet on the picket lines. Not a shot was fired. When the band, just to our rear, played, "The Star Spangled Banner," a band on the rebel line played, "The Bonny Blue Flag," and the concert began. We played "Hail Columbia," and were answered by "Dixie." "Rally 'Round the Flag" was followed by "Palmetto State." Then came "John Brown's Body," which brought out "My Old Kentucky Home." When both bands struck up with "Home, Sweet Home," and not a shot was fired all the evening.

—133—

Leaving the 20th Corps to take care of Atlanta, we moved in the direction of Macon, destroying the railroad as we went, reaching Jonesboro, September 1st. That battle was fought principally by Thomas's corps. Our division was most fortunate in regard to position. The battle really was fought by massing our artillery in such a position as to rake the trenches of the enemy. We formed in a ravine sloping to the west, and charged through a field of standing corn. Capt. Hutchinson pushed out the skirmish line, while we followed up to the works. The column on our left seemed to merge into our line, over the breast works and down into the trenches, up to the battery on the eminence above, we went. They had no time to spike the guns. We turned them on the retreating foe to the right. Our capture consisted of sixteen guns, part of which had been taken from McPherson's men on the 22nd of July, and thirteen hundred prisoners, a whole Texas brigade. One of the Texas rangers refused to surrender, and had raised his gun to shoot an officer of the 86th Illinois, when a yankee felled him with a stroke of his empty musket, and saved the officer's life. The loss in our regiment was light, five killed, Henry Bargar and Robert N. Mercer, Co. B; Alfred Brister, Co. C; James W. Sheets, Co. E, and J. B. McCarrol, Co. G. There were nineteen wounded. Major Holmes was slightly wounded in the knee, but was in the saddle in a few days. James W. Sheets, who had been fearfully torn by a hand shell, at Kenesaw, and had returned the day before the battle. He was a brave soldier, having followed the retreating rebels, was shot while between the lines, behind a tree.

The 17th New York, of the 1st Division, suffered in the the charge. They wore red turban caps, which made an excellent mark for the enemy. The enemy lost heavily. Over six hundred of their dead were buried the next day. This battle settled the fate of Atlanta. That night, dispirited and defeated, the city was evacuated. They destroyed their surplus ammunition, loading it on cars and running them outside of the city, setting fire to them. It sounded like a terrific bombardment to us. The midnight glow of burning cotton and supplies could be seen by us, as it lighted Hood, fleeing with his army toward Macon.

"Atlanta is ours—their own Gate City, and fairly won," said Sherman, and his great campaign was ended.

For grandeur of design, depth and skill of combination, it stands unrivalled in militaty history. Now we are to rest awhile. We moved toward Atlanta the morning of the 4th, guarding 1600 prisoners, mostly Texas troops. They were not typical southerners. Many of them were from the north, but they declared "they would die in the last ditch," and never give up.

Col. "Bill" Thompson, of the 8th Texas, was a fine looking fellow, with a genial face, and in his capture he had exhibited a reckless bravery. We found him at one of the deserted guns with his coat off, loading the gun with grape shot. He asked us for Muskingum county boys, and we learned that he was a son of James Thompson, of Adamsville, that county, and that we had known him before he went south. He was an unreconstructed rebel, declaring he was in the rebel army to stay until the south had won.

We arrived at Atlanta, glad to be unmolested by sounds of war, or visions of blood and death. We had our first dress parade in four months, the next evening after our arrival.

"All present or accounted for," said the orderly sergeants. More were to be accounted for than were present. My own company started out May 6th, with 63 men and officers, and we stacked seventeen guns when we arrived in Atlanta, Sept. 4th, the company commanded by Sergeant E Tappan Hamlon, who died in April, 1900, at Hebron, Nebraska, ticketed all the way through.

Our losses in the one hundred and twenty days' fighting, and two hundred and fifty miles marching, including the shifting of troops from one end of the line to the other, was, according to Surgeon Henry M. Duff's memorandum, commissioned officers killed, 4; wounded, 13; enlisted men, 54; wounded 169. Four officers and forty men died of wounds, total 102 killed or died of wounds and 138 wounded. From a careful search of the records and correspondence there were 29 men wounded, not reported, mostly slight wounds, not found in the list reported by the surgeon.

Your historian was wounded August 17th, in front of Atlanta, and was by mistake taken to 1st Division hospital, after night, and thus failed to be reported by our surgeon in his private memoranda.

Our loss was 102 killed or died of wounds; 167 wounded and recovered, and twenty captured, total 289.

CAPT. PETER C. SCHNEIDER, CO. I.

CHAPTER XIII.

RESTING IN ATLANTA AND FOREST'S RAID.

WE are now in Atlanta, which had, at the breaking out of the war, a population of ten thousand. It was the county seat of Fulton county, and now the capitol of the state. The city is about eleven hundred feet above sea level, and laid out in the form of a circle, the diameter, at the time we entered, being two miles. We are here for rest, but there was no rest for us.

We dug a well fifty-seven feet deep and found splendid water. We were ordered to have two roll calls every day, and the orderly could be heard, going up and down the company street, in the morning, singing to the tune of the reveille, "I can't get them up, I can't get them up, I can't get them up in the morning!" and was compelled to abandon the task.

A lively cricket of a newspaper appeared, in place of the "Memphis Avalanche," that had moved with the rebel host. With the daily came the newsboy, who, a week before, had been curled up in a store box in Cincinnatti. The same shrewd, sharp urchin that jumps into his clothes, and runs out into the world, with a shell on his back like a quail, or resembled a shell bark hickory nut, more cover than kernel. The morning air rang with "Here's your mornin' paper."

We drank of the well and waited for the good news by mail from God's country. It came. Poor old John Morgan had been killed by Gillam's men. What a tragic death. Then Sheridan's ride up the Shenandoah valley was announced, and three cheers and a tiger for "Phil and his "Black-charger."

How we made the old camp ring, when Col. Clancy and the boys captured at Peach Tree came in, and the regiment began to look like itself again. Only eight officers were present for duty up to this time, namely, Holmes, Brice, Rothacker, Hutchinson, Armstrong, Summers, James and Duff.

We left Atlanta by train to intercept Forest, who was raiding in Tennessee. We arrived at Chattanooga once more, and look upon things that are familiar. As the sun rose, we thought before us are the monuments of deeds that shall outlast the house of the grave maker. Almost a year before, the curtains of heaven were lifted, and God thundered at the battlements of the enemy of liberty, and they crumbled. Now, ranks of corn had ripened along these acres, and we said "How swift the plough share follows the sword." Think of it! Where, last November, we saw Hooker move up to battle in the clouds, with his stout and steady legions, now the farmer was gathering up along the base of that mountain his bountiful crop of potatoes. How ugly the scrawl of war's wild fingers has marred this beautiful world of ours. Yet we forget its deadly work. As we passed down the Tennessee we saw the old time flowers growing, like they used to do in my mother's garden. The sun flowers and the holly-hock, where the little negroes used to bag many a bee to hear "its small and mellow horn." So homelike and sheltered by those valleys were the houses that we forgot we knew the time that death lurked in every footstep. We pursued our journey to Shoal's creek, six miles from Florence, and found that Forest had crossed the river going south. After resting two days we turned our faces backwards, bound, as we supposed, for Atlanta again

Taking the train at Athens, we landed in Chattanooga Oct. 14, to find great excitement over the report that Hood was marching on the place, while we could hear nothing of Sherman. We pushed right on, passing the old Chickamauga battle field, through Lafayette and Alpine to Gaylesville, Alabama, five miles from the Coosa river. Sherman and the whole army seemed to be there. Hood had gone "where the woodbine twineth."

Atlanta was safe and we were to take a few days' rest. Sherman had decided to send the 4th and 23rd corps to watch Hood, and Thomas went back to Nashville to organize an army and drive him to the Gulf, while the rest of "uncle Billy's" boys turned their faces towards Atlanta.

At Kingston the paymaster gave us eight month's dues, and we sent Capt. Rothacker with a guard to Chattanooga to express the money home, Company E sending twenty-seven hundred dollars. Many of the boys lost the whole of their hard earned wages around the faro banks and chuck-luck boards. Many arrests were made by Sherman's provost guard, while three officers lost their shoulder straps for gambling with the men.

November 8th was Presidential election day. We were on the march, but were halted by the way and proceeded to cast our ballots, either for Abraham Lincoln or Geo. B. McClellan. Hutchinson, Grimes and Lane were the Judges, and we deposited our ballots by the roadside. The 52nd gave Lincoln 182 and McClellan 32, while the 98th Ohio gave Lincoln 212 and McClellan 17. Lincoln was elected, having 212 electoral votes to McClellan's 21, for the 2nd term. Allowing 100 men to the regiment, that were too young to vote, this would give the strength of the regiment at 325 men.

Everything seemed to be going towards Atlanta, yet we could not see why we were destroying the railroad, our source of supplies, but we pondered these things in our hearts until we arrived at Atlanta.

Orders came for each man to draw two pairs of shoes and to be ready for a long march, having a complete soldier's outfit, which consisted of a haversack, canteen, woolen blanket, rubber blanket, one-half of a "dog tent," a knapsack and an extra shirt, besides what he had on his back. Sherman had rapidly concentrated here 60,000, thoroughly organized and equipped men. Forty-one men had come up from the hospitals to swell our ranks, and we were ready.

Everything of use to the rebel army had been destroyed at Rome, and Atlanta. Sherman wrote to Admiral Porter to be on the lookout for him about Christmas, and to his wife, "This is my last letter, you will hear from me through rebel sources." The army consisted of four corps and two wings, the right and left. Gen. Howard commanding the right and Slocum the left wing, with two divisions of cavalry commanded by Gen. Kilpatrick. The columns were to start regularly at six o'clock every morning for an average march of fifteen miles a day.

When Sherman made public this daring movement, both North and South were astonished. The rebel editors proclaimed the destruction of Sherman's army. In Europe it created equal astonishment. The Richmond papers scornfully said that his march would lead him to the paradise of fools.

Sherman knew what he was doing. He cut loose from his moorings, and drifted boldly out to sea. By the road Slocum was to take it was 170 miles to Augusta. By that on which Howard marched it was 291 to Savannah. His army train consisted of about four thousand vehicles of all kinds, which if stretched in a single line, would have extended forty miles. We carried forty days' rations of hard tack, coffee, sugar and salt. The rest we expected to find laying around loose as we journeyed. Very few seemed to dread the trip. We had something new every day. Nerve centers were touched, our march was to send a thrill through the entire army of the Union and make the loyal North proud of the army of the west as they went "Marching through Georgia," sweeping like an avalanche to the sea. We began to speculate as to how we would live off the country, and too, we thought how our friends would pity us as they heard we were living on alligators, with pipe clay and stump water for a change. We did not expect to see the delicate bones of many quail about the camp, or hear of oysters on the half-shell, but we grew eloquent when we thought of the land, flowing with sorghum and sweet potatoes. While thus discussing the march, our band struck up "When the Cruel War is Over," and then played, "Oh, Take Your Time Miss Lucy." Then we laid us down in a soldiers' bed to dream of yams and other good things.

CAPT. HENRY O. MANSFIELD, CO. E.

CHAPTER XIV.

ON Wednesday morning, November 16th, our splendid army of brawny western men, stripped like an athlete for the race, set its face toward the Atlantic ocean, with banners streaming and bands playing, we bade farewell to the smoldering ruins of Atlanta.

It was two in the afternoon when Baldwin put the bugle to his lips and struck up, "John Brown's Body," the full band made the earth tremble, while, with a sort of a "don't care" swing we marched out, the last regiment, the rear guard, in charge of our division wagon train. Water was very scarce, and we were late in going into camp, having made eleven miles.

The second day's march led us along the Georgia railroad which we effectually destroyed, Passing through Lythonia the next day, we came to one of the greatest natural curiosities in the state. An isolated stone mountain, formed of one solid rock, nearly twenty-two hundred feet high and seven miles around its base. From the summit there is a fine view of the surrounding country. A dead Union soldier was found near here with this notice pinned upon his breast, "Death to all foragers," and while we looked into his face, the inward monitor whispered, "cruel war."

Our march next day led us through Newton county, almost in the center of the state. The sweet potato crop of this county was estimated at four hundred thousand bushels. These had been gathered and stored away for shipment to the rebel army. As we passed along we took our choice between the yellow nassemond and the red yams. We were ordered to forage liberally, aiming to keep in the wagons ten days' rations for the horses and men. Soldiers were not allowed to enter the dwellings of those who stayed at home, or commit any trespass, but they were permitted to gather turnips, potatoes and other vegetables, and to drive in stock, wherever they were found. Most of the whites fled before us with the rebel cavalry, and where we found their homes deserted, we gathered everything that was eatable.

As we moved out for the day's march, you might see, here and there, strange pets on whom the owners lavished their affections, which were little touches of the gentler nature, which may be seen today, with old soldiers, in the clasp of the friendly hand. We often thought that the tenderest care did not come from the recruit, fresh from home and its endearments, but from the rough, battle-scarred men, generous fellows, long cherished in memory. One of the boys carried a red squirrel more than two thousand miles. "Bun" ate hard tack like a veteran. Another's affections were lavished on a little booby owl, bearing the classical name of Minerva. One had a pet bear. But chief among camp pets were dogs. On the saddles, in the baggage wagons, growling under a cannon, yellow at that, and pug nosed, with old names, such as "Tray" and "Towser," "Blanche" and "Caesar." A dog, like a horse, came to like the rattle and crash of musketry and cannon. There was one in an Illinois regiment that would chase a half spent shot at Kenesaw, like a kitten would play with a ball. He had been twice wounded, and left the tip of his tail at Stone River. An Illinois battery had a little white spaniel that delighted in the name of "Dot." He always messed with the boys and had his silken coat washed every day. When crossing a stream one day they put him into the sponge bucket that swung under the rear axle, put the cover on, as they always had for a ride. Nobody thought of "Dot." When all was over, a gunner looked into the bucket and "Dot" was as dead as a dirty door mat. Many will remember "Old Abe," the war eagle, of the 8th Wisconsin. He was captured by Captain Perkins and presented to the regiment, where he shared the fortunes of war until the regiment veteraned, when he was left with the Adjutant General of the State at Madison, where he remained until the close of the war.

We pushed on through Eatonton, Newton County, and turning southward, headed for Milledgeville.

It turned cold. The ground was slightly frozen in the morning. With the bracing morning air, we started out, the band playing "Dixie," and the boys began to sing

> "Hoe de corn and scratch de grabble
> In Dixie's land I'se bound to trabble."

And we did scratch gravel, for we arrived at Milledgeville before twelve o'clock, having made sixteen miles.

Eli B. Barnes of Co. F, lost his pocket book and one of Howell Cobb's slaves, an old farm hand, found it and returned it to him It contained $25. Gen. Cobb was not at home, but we made ourselves at home, anyway. His slaves were packing their bundles to follow Sherman, and we never shall forget the advice of "Old Jimmy." White-haired and bent with the toil of a slave, he stood upon the auction block where many of his race had been sold as cattle, and grew eloquent as he said, "De year ob Jubilee is come, and Massa Linkum will come along some day and say, 'you's free,' " and advised them to stay at home and not burden Massa Sherman with "de women and children to feed."

We believe they took his advice, as few left the plantation when we moved onward. Gen. Cobb was then in his prime, 49, and a rabid secessionist, and never was reconstructed. He died suddenly while on a visit to New York in 1868.

Milledgeville was the capitol of the state. When we entered it, it had a population of about two thousand, and was situated about eighty-five miles south-east of Atlanta. The soldiers took possession of the State House, on Clark street, organizing the legislature with a representative from the one hundred and thirty-six counties of the state. They elected a speaker, and proceeded to business. The first act passed was the repeal of the ordinance of secession. Some of the finest speeches we ever listened to were made on that floor. Parliamentary rules may have been violated, yet the proceedings were much more interesting and sensible than what had taken place the day before, when the rebels fled in haste for their homes. Here we saw the degrading curse of American slavery. A man as white as any Yank said to us: "Massa's with Gen. McGruder, Missus and I runs this hotel." The planter saw that humanity was profitable, not always with a black skin. With his dogs, horses, and gun, his wines and dinners to attract those whose society he courted, he lived to perpetuate the foul curse of African servitude, and every true American soldier felt called of God with fire and sword to blot the iniquity from the land.

The Third National Thanksgiving of war time was observed near here, in true New England style. Not with the clamor of camp life, but with thanks to God for what he was doing for us.

Fighting began soon after we left Milledgeville. At Sandersville several were wounded, and Anthony Hartley of Co. D was taken prisoner at Fenn's Bridge. The boys of Co. D did not fare so well when Anthony was gone. He was a great forager.

Fifteen miles from the Savannah river we turned south, following the only railroad running to Savannah, until we reached Millen. The Union prisoners had been removed from Andersonville to this place about four weeks previous, but they were hastily removed from Millen ten days before we arrived. Two dead bodies were found, unburied, which they had left in their haste to get away.

Our march toward Savannah was rapid. The road was wide, and cavalry and infantry were massed together, cavalry in the center and infantry as escort, on the sides of the road. Sometimes bands of music answering each other in the distance, filled the vast forest with melody. Following us was a tattered crowd of blacks, that, despite Sherman's order, followed on our trail. When we came to the black swamp we lifted our pontoons, and left them on the other side. Somehow they crossed that night, overtaking us the next day.

We halted near Ebenezer Church, noted as having been occupied by General Washington during the Revolutionary War, and John Wesley, the founder of Methodism, had preached there when a missionary to the colonies. Here Major Holmes was compelled to fall back on "Jocko," his famous war horse. The Major bought "Jocko" from the Colonel of the 12th Iowa, at Kingston, just before we left Atlanta. He, had bought him from a Mississippi planter. The planter bought him from the Comanche Indians. He was perfectly white when foaled—a rare thing—and had some marks of the Arabian pony, and some of the Mexican broncho, but was always greater than these. He made his mile in three minutes under the saddle. We first saw him at the battle of Mission Ridge, as Smith's division charged over the tunnel. He carried a scar made by a piece of shell, at Vicksburg. Major Holmes mounted him on the Carolina march with more than a hundred horses of the battalion, he led in protecting the men who gathered food for the second division, and when we reached Goldsboro, N. C., every horse that had left Savannah with the squadron had been left, abandoned or killed, but "Jocko," He had covered fifty miles a day most of the time, and came into Goldsboro without a chafe, puff or scar, the best piece of horseflesh I ever saw, his-strength, endurance and intelligence being marvelous. He brought "Jocko" home with him. On the 6th of July, 1892, on the banks of Alum Creek, Franklin county, O., seven miles from Columbus, on the farm of W. T. Rees, he accidently broke his leg, and died with his boots on. An old soldier decently buried him with military honors at the age of thirty-two.

Hardee resisted our approach to Savannah by planting torpedoes in the road, felling trees and occasionally shelling our advance. It was here that Lieut. Coe of Barnett's battery was killed by a shell. One of Nature's noblemen, Major Holmes, said to me: "His face made a sun spot on my heart, and, like the scent of the roses about the broken vase, will hang around it for many a year."

Barnett's battery was recruited in Central Illinois in '61 by Capt. Chas. W. Keith. He was succeeded by Chas. M. Barnett, and he by Judson Rich. They were lucky in having but one officer killed, and twenty men wounded, during the war.

The first rations of hard tack was issued on Dec. 12th. We had lived for ten days on rice, which we found in abundance stacked in the fields. We shelled it and hulled it in an iron pot, with an oval bottom for a mortar, and a bayonet for a pestle. We cooked it with fresh beef chopped fine, and ate it as the chinaman eats soup—without the chopsticks.

Fort McCallister was taken by General Hazen's men in a gallant charge, and communications were opened at the mouth of the Ogeechee. "Come and get your mail," shouted Ross Rex, on the morning of the 17th, and you might have seen "an eager, anxious throng, pressing the busy street along." How anxious! "Good news from a far country."

Thirty six days before, we had received our last mail at Kingston. Thomas had whipped Hood at Nashville, and all things were moving toward the end, and friends at home were happy and well.

Sherman entered Savannah and sent Lincoln the following dispatch, "Here's your Christmas gift, the city of Savannah, 13 locomotives, 35 thousand bales of cotton, and one hundred thousand bushels of rice."

We are to rest. This campaign stands alone in the history of modern warfare. The south was dumbfounded. The north was jubilant with delight. Our army in good condition. Not a wagon lost. My own company came into Savannah with every man we had when we left Atlanta. Wonderful march! The world will never cease wondering at its magnitude, originality and success.

We ate our Christmas dinner in Savannah. Our first Christmas in the army was spent in Nashville. The second at North Chickamauga, and the third where the robbins were almost as thick as house flies. They awoke us every morning with their song of "chir-up, cheer-up." Christmas came on Sunday and we went to St. John's Episcopal church and heard George W. Pepper, Chaplain of the 80th Ohio, preach. It was a remarkable sermon. I suppose he did his best as Gen. Sherman and his staff were present. I had always wanted to hear the man who had preached one Sunday morning in sixty-one, in Warsaw, Coshocton county, O., and enrolled a company for the war before he left the church. As we returned from church we could easily see that the stranger was within the gates. A ceaseless turbulent stream of all colors and kinds of humanity crowded the thoroughfares. Look which way you would, you could see stars. No doubt many of the boys in blue turned their eyes to the north and thought of home and of the last struggle. There came to us the words of Prentice.

"Remorseless time, fierce spirit of the glass and scythe,
What power can stay thine onward course or melt thine iron heart to pity."

In one of our battles in the south, a white dove bewildered by the thunder, flew in and out amid the clouds of the battle, and at last fluttered, panting, down upon the wheel of a gun. It was a strange place for the emblem of peace. It belonged to the white flag, and not to the red. An artillery man captured it in his powder-stained hands, caressed it a moment and freed it, in an instant it was lost in the storm. Had that bird flown with the captor's thought, can you doubt it would have fluttered at last at the window of the gunner's far-off home.

"We must not tarry," said Sherman, as he spoke of his third and final campaign. He still has sixty-five thousand men. The distance to be traveled before the army should reach its objective point—Goldsboro, was about five hundred miles. His men were in the best of spirits. Thomas had scattered Hood. Grant and Sherman could now cooperate and crush out the last armed foe. There is to be a few changes in the officers. Logan has joined us and is in command of his old corps. Physically he was one of the finest officers in the army. A deep and fierce black eye, a very dark complexion, which gave him the name of "Black-Jack." Howard is still in command of the left. He was known as the "Christian Soldier." At Fair Oaks he lost his right arm and is still living, the same soldier, for God and humanity.

Lieut. Colonel J. W. Langley was relieved of the command of McCook's brigade and Brigadier General B. D. Fehring was to lead us through the Carolinas. He had won his star at Chickamauga, while leading his regiment, the 92nd Ohio. He was a brave officer, and being tidy in his dress, made a fine appearance as a commanding officer.

We failed in our attempt to cross into South Carolina, opposite Savannah, on account of the heavy rains, as the low rice fields were badly flooded. We left Savannah the 21st of January and reached Sister's Ferry, sixty miles up the Savannah river, on the Georgia side, on the 29th. The heavy rains had made the river almost three miles wide at the Ferry, and we were compelled to wait until Feb. 5th. Three divisions of the 14th corps—one of the 20th, and Gen. Kilpatrick with his cavalry were waiting to cross. Sherman with the right wing and two divisions of the 20th corps were moving in the direction of the Charleston and Augusta railroad.

FIRST SERGT. ABRAHAM R. HOLMES, CO. G.

CHAPTER XV.

THE gunboat "Pontiac," commanded by Captain Luce, had come up to cover our crossing. The cold winter rains had set in, and the roads were in a terrible condition, but we managed to dry our clothes before the camp fire, and crawling into our "dog tent," went to sleep in a moment, a slumber so near akin to death, that the orderly had to shake each man to wake him, even after the bugle had sounded the morning call.

Providence seemed against us in starting, but we crossed the pontoon bridge. As we got out into the middle of the river, we could more easily understand why an eccentric father named his daughter "Savannah." It was a beautiful thing that girl was named for. The trees that lined its banks were festooned with Spanish Moss, hung like the curtains of the old "Tabernacle," which Moses built, while sojourning in the wilderness. The night encampments were gloomy and cold. With the morning light, the bugle call roused us, alike in stormy and pleasant weather. As we pushed on over the dreary country, our feelings were very much changed, the moment we set foot on South Carolina soil. Not a house or fence was left standing, along our march. The state was the first to pass the ordinance of secession, and fire upon the old flag, and to make the feeling more intense, Hampton's cavalry began to kill all men caught away from their commands. Sherman selected ten men by lot from the prisoners in his hands, and shot them in retaliation.

Our second day's march brought us to the Salkehatchie river at Brighton, Hampton county. Here we destroyed the

Charleston and Augusta railroad, thus dividing the rebel forces at Charleston from those concentrating at Augusta. Crossing the Edisto, straight through the heart of the proud rebellious state, the mighty columns moved with resistless power, until on the tenth, we were in Blackwell, Barnwell county.

Sherman has never received justice for his strategy in deceiving the enemy as to his movements, by which he cut, effectually, their lines of communication, preventing the uniting of their forces, whereby they might have harassed our march all through the state. The left wing had no communication with the right wing except by couriers, until we reached Columbia, yet we could follow their line of march, by the dark cloud of smoke made by burning cotton gins and outbuildings. Kilpatrick said to Sherman as we started "How shall I let you know where I am?" "Oh, just burn a barn or something and make a smoke, as the Indians do on the plains," was Sherman's reply. The smoke of the burning pine forests was so dense that we yankees were almost as black as coal heavers, or the negroes that followed us. Forage was scarce. One of our boys, who had tramped all day and "caught nothing," said to us, "South Carolina seems to have but two staple commodities, frogs and bad roads," while we had two equals to balance the condition of affairs, stomachs and haversacks, both empty.

A detail of foragers sent out from the Edisto river, after two days search for the fat of the land, took an inventory of what they had gathered as follows: One cart, with a broken wheel; one yoke of oxen, red and brindle; one peck of sweet potatoes, one-half to an inch thick; one rooster, too old to crow and a half bushel of wilted turnips.

Columbia was taken by the 25th Iowa, Colonel Stone commanding, Wade Hampton retreating. It was a mystery to me why the enemy made no resistance. Columbia is on the Congaree river at the junction of the Saluda and Broad, which is navigable to this point. The capital is one hundred miles northwest of Charleston. It was a beautiful city, built on a plain 200 feet above the river, and its streets are one hundred feet wide. The city was burned by firing the cotton bales, which had been piled on the street corners, in their attempt to get it loaded on trains for transportation to Charleston, The cotton was fired by the rebel cavalry. A strong wind blew the burning mass to all parts of the city and no effort could save it. Twenty-five blocks went up in flames. When Colonel Stone's men entered the city, they found twenty-seven Union prisoners, which had been hidden by an old negro in the loft of an unoccupied church building. They had escaped while they were being taken to Saulsbury prison. They came out from their hiding place to greet the old flag, and sent up cheer after cheer for Sherman.

Our division did not enter Columbia, but many of the boys crossed in a flatboat that night, and took in the sights and scenes of the burning city. We marched unmolested northward. The 20th corps crossed the Catawba at Hanging Rock, while the 14th corps crossed a little lower down, on the road to Chesterfield. The pontoon bridge was torn from its moorings by the swollen river and it was with difficulty that we were enabled to replace it, but we succeeded after a day and night of anxiety and made up the lost time by marching twenty-five miles a day until we crossed the North Carolina line at Sneedsboro, on the Great Pee Dee river. We had drawn two pairs of shoes, when we started. They proved to be worthless, for as soon as the threads were cut, they were soleless Marching in the sand of that dense pine region, our feet being ground with the grains of sand, we were compelled to ask for a mount, and travel as a scout with a number of others, who hung upon the flank of our columns. In the role of a scout, with two others, we came to a cross-roads Desiring to keep in safe distance from the marching column, we halted for counsel. A citizen drove up in a one-horse vehicle. He proved to be the mail carrier from Cheraw to Jacksonville, the county seat of Onslow county. Taking charge of the mail, we traded horses with him, also our government shoes for a "two-hundred dollar pair of boots," giving seventy-five dollars, confederate money, to make it even. Taking the mail to General Slocum's headquarters, we were complimented for the capture.

Moving rapidly toward Fayetteville, we were two days passing through the dense pine forests of North Carolina, expecting to reach Fayetteville, on the Cape Fear river, by the 10th of March. Our progress was necessarily slow on account of a large force of cavalry in our front, stubbornly resisting our advance, in order to let Johnson concentrate on the east side of the Cape Fear river.

Kilpatrick was surprised in his camp by Wade Hampton, before day on the morning of the 9th—and we made a forced march of six miles to help him out. But brave "Kill" brought victory out of defeat, and drove Hampton toward the river. A large turpentine factory had been fired by Hampton's men to keep its valuable stores from falling into our hands. It was a terrible conflagration. One of the boys of Co. D, in describing the fire to a group of eager listeners, after he came home, said, "The blaze rose four miles toward heaven, leaping and roaring like a bursting volcano. So great was the heat from the burning casks and tar pits, that we were compelled to turn to the right eight miles down Fallis creek, crossing at a ford, the water being so hot from the heated air of the mighty burning cauldron, that it took the hair off the horse's legs as they forded it."

The foragers of the 15th corps, under command of Major Holmes, drove the cavalry out of Fayetteville on the morning of the eleventh, but were too late to save the fine bridge over the Cape Fear river. The gun boat, Davidson, Captain Ainsworth commanding, reached Fayetteville a few hours after our men captured it, opening communications with Wilmington by the river. Fayetteville was the county seat of Cumberland county and had a population of six thousand. The United States Arsenal had been removed from Harper's Ferry, Va., to this place a year or two before the war began. When the first shot was fired on Fort Sumpter it was taken possession of by the rebels, in it was stored thirty-five thousand stand of arms and a number of cannon. In 1870 the city had twenty prosperous churches. The citizens were glad to see us and said, "we are tired of this cruel war."

Slocum crossed at Fayetteville. Howard three miles below, on the fifteenth. Raleigh was fifty-five miles north of us, and we expected to meet the combined armies of Johnson and Hardee somewhere in the near future where a battle would decide the fate of the campaign. Taking the plank road to Raleigh on the morning of the fifteenth we encountered Hardee eleven miles north, near Kyle's landing. On the morning of the sixteenth, Ward's division of the 20th corps encountered the enemy, entrenched a mile and a half from Averysboro, a small village in Harnet county. The ground was so swampy that it was almost impossible to get our artillery in position. The 14th corps formed on the left of the 20th, near the Cape Fear river. Rhett's heavy artillery from Charleston were in front of us. Col. Rhett was captured early in the day by our skirmishers. The enemy had three small black cannon, six pounders. A shot from Winnager's battery on our line exploded in one of the lumber chests killing every one of the battery horses attached to it. Caskey's Brigade of Ward's division made a brilliant charge on the left and rear, capturing the battery and two hundred and seventy prisoners. The South Carolina boys fled in confusion leaving guns, blankets and knapsacks in the trenches. We pushed the enemy a mile or more finding a line of works more substantially constructed. Slowly and steadily we crept up on their line encountering fierce opposition. We lost three killed and seven wounded. The brave and genial Capt. James M. Summers commanding Co. D, fell mortally wounded while charging the enemy in the morning, and is buried at Newberne, North Carolina. Wm. M. Flemming of the trio of Flemming brothers, Company B, was killed on the line and is buried at Raleigh. Rob't M. Blackburn of Co. E was pierced on the first line and was buried where he fell, before we advanced in the evening. He was a good soldier, quiet and lovable in his disposition. He served just one year. Geo. S. Thomas of Company E, was disabled by a gun shot wound, through the hand. He lives in Scio, O. We lost in this battle, seventy-seven killed, and four hundred and seventy-seven wounded. The rebels left one hundred and eighty-five dead on the field, which we buried, they retreating toward Smithfield.

We moved at ten in the morning of the 18th. Marching fourteen miles, camping five miles from Bentonville, in Johnson county, and twenty-seven miles from Goldsboro. Only two more days and the goal would be reached. Carlin's division of our corps took the lead the next morning. Our bummers, who were known as mounted foragers, encountered Dibbrell's cavalry and easily drove them back. But they were amazed to run into a line of infantry, entrenched. Prisoners taken by Major Holmes' mounted scouts, reported Johnson in front with three corps, respectively commanded by Hoke, Hardee and Cheatham, numbering about thirty thousand men.

Johnson pushed out and attacked the head of our column, gaining temporary advantage, driving the two leading brigades back to the main body. General Sherman had spent the night with Slocum, but had started early in the morning to join the right wing, four miles south.

There was a lull in the fighting for some lttle time, when Slocum deployed the two divisions of our corps, Morgan's and Carlin's, Beard being in the rear guarding the wagon train. The 20th corps marched rapidly into position, and the artillery was massed on a knoll a little to the rear of our works.

No one who took part in that battle can forget the thick, dark growth of pines that lifted their heads from a morass almost impassable, nor the stern determination with which our line went forward through the pathless swamp to meet an unseen enemy hid from all view, until his ringing musketry told us we had found his hiding place. Our batteries did splendid service. They thrust their ponderous fists into the face of the enemy, planting blows at will.

All that saved us from crushing defeat, was the dense pine thicket which held Johnson at bay, until our scattered forces came up. Fehring's brigade, to which we belonged, occupied three positions during the fight. Our first position was on the right, and in the rear of Vandever's brigade, where we commenced a line of works, but were moved to the left and front of Mitchell's brigade, and across the road on which we came in from Averysboro. Our second position was at least five hundred yards in front of the line on which the battle was fought in the afternoon.

At noon the enemy left their works and made their first desperate charge. Gen. Davis rode out to our line and moved us back on a line with Mitchell, but there was a gap between us and Mitchell. Vandever was brought up and still there was a gap, and Slocum ordered Cogswell's brigade of the 20th Corps to come in between us and Vandever. When the assault was made, our line was as follows: Mitchell on the extreme right, Vandever, then Cogswell, then Fehring, then Miles, Hobart and Robinson, with Dustan's and Case's brigades of the 20th corps in the reserve. The first assault was made against Fehring and Cogswell, Hardee and Hoke led the charge. They came through the woods with arms trailed, firing but little, as if they determined to crush our line by mere might of numbers. But we met them with volley after volley, mowing them down like grass, but they bowed their heads and came on. They penetrated between Cogswell and Mitchell, yet neither gave way. Mitchell had a strong barricade of pine logs, and he would repulse them on one side, climb over and fight those that were in his rear.

The 98th Ohio came out of the fight with a record unequaled by any regiment, in that unequal contest with Johnson's Veterans. More than a score of that regiment deserved remembrance for gallantry at the hands of the government.

We had fought Johnson before on many a contested field. Here we whipped him for the last time. He was repulsed on all sides. His dead were found on four sides of Mitchell's brigade, in the rear and front of Vandever and Fehring. They fought with spirit and determination. Their line was relieved three times, and fresh troops sent in, but we were in our last battle of Sherman's bold adventure and we must drive the rebels from their last ditch. In this battle our line received six distinct assaults by the combined forces of Johnson's three corps.

For the time it lasted, Bentonville was the most sanguinary battle of the war, and the only serious one between Atlanta and Raleigh. Sherman expected this battle, but did not intend to have it thrown on Slocum alone. In successive waves, column after column came with a determination to carry our works at any sacrifice. But right in their path was "Pap Thomas'" old corps, the 14th, now led by Jeff C. Davis.

I can give you but a faint idea of the battle cauldron that boiled in that dense thicket of pines. An incident here and there will assist you in painting the picture for yourself. The dead were on both sides of our works. Guns and scabbards, dead horses, and wrecks of abulances, that had been left in the swamp. Bloody garments and bloody men strewed the ground, and, tread lightly, for the boys, who saved the day are lying there. No more they cheer, as they charged or fought hand to hand over those pine logs and never for them, sweet as heaven itself, will the soldier return to home and friends.

Our loss was light, perhaps the lightest of any battle in which we were engaged for the amount of firing we did. I verily believe that the 98th Ohio killed more of the enemy than that regiment reported for duty the morning of the battle. We lay flat upon the ground, until the enemy were within thirty yards of us, concealed by the dense undergrowth, when we arose, poured a volley into their faces, and then charged them in their confusion. We were on the skirmish line most of the morning and were taken in by one of their charges, but the 17th New York of the first division charged their flank and recaptured us in a short time after our capture.

Sherman's entire loss was twenty-three officers and fifteen hundred and eighty-one men, while Johnson officially reported twenty-three hundred and forty-three. The loss in the regiment, killed and mortally wounded, six, and twenty three wounded. Six of my own company were absent from roll call. Sergeant David M. Scott lost an arm. We helped to take him to the hospital, where he watched the surgeon take off the mangled limb, as calm as he had gone into battle an hour before. John F. Rightly lived an hour after he was carried from the field. Joseph M. Thompson, who fell with me at Linnville, was seriously wounded in the thigh, but he still lives. Robert Farrow of Co. D, was killed early in the day. Peter Risser of Co. I was mortally wounded in the charge in the afternoon.

General Ben D. Fehring was wounded in the hand early in the afternoon and the command fell upon Lieut. Col. Langley of the 125th Ill. Gen. Fehring was a brave officer. By his kindness and gentlemanly bearing he was beloved and respected by all the men. He died in Marietta, Ohio, shortly after the war.

Howard came up in the night and we were safe. We spent the night where we had fought through the day with the dead all around us. Men, prone upon their faces in death's deep abasement,—here lies one, his head pillowed upon his folded arms, there one, his cheek pressed upon a stone as was Jacob's at Bethel, yonder one with his fingers stiffened round a musket—over yonder a butternut and a true blue had gone down together, the arm of one flung over the other. We pass on to where a lieutenant grasps a bush as if he died vainly feeling for a little hold upon earth and life.

Those faces are not what you would think they would be. Not one of them distorted with any passion, but white and calm, as if in dream of peace, still a few strangely beautiful. As we visited the hospital next day, to see how the boys were coming on, the floor all around was one layer deep with wounded men. Bandages, white and ghastly, everywhere. Bandages, bandages, with now and then a rusty spot of blood.

Only a day off that bloody field, and yet what worn-out, faded faces look up at you. A jolly Irishman from the 17th New York (those fellows that wore the red turbans,) had lost his right arm. One of the nurses was complaining that things were not going to please him, when Pat said to him,—"I tell you, man, shut up your growling, or I'll knock you down wish my stump." That was their last battle.

Johnson did not leave our front. He only changed his lines to protect his left. We charged their picket line, driving them in just in front of us, and set fire to an old vacant house, where a number of sharpshooters had concealed themselves. That night quiet reigned along the line, until shortly after eight, when General Mitchell, who commanded the 1st division of our corps, worn out with anxiety and worry of the battle, laid down with one of his men for a little sleep, when an officer of his staff aroused him saying, "Here is a staff officer with a message for you." He arose and met a bright young fellow, who said, "Col. Hardee presents his compliments to you and asks that you will apprise your line, that he is forming in your front, to charge the Yankee lines on your left." Gen. Mitchell asked him to repeat his message—which he did. The General inquired, "what Colonel it was," and was told, "Colonel Hardee of the 23rd Georgia."

Mitchell sent the young man to the rear, called in his entire picket line, waited until the rebel line was formed in his front, and at the tap of a drum, a volley was fired into the rebel lines, followed by screams and groans, and cursings. The next morning, among the dead was found a line of new Enfield rifles, just from England, and knapsacks almost as straight as if laid out for a Sunday morning inspection.

Col. Hardee, who was severely wounded, told some of our officers, "that his men had never been in battle, and had not fired a gun in the two days previous, and when they were brought out to make that attack, they had boasted they would go right over the Yankee works, and vowed they would take no prisoners." They had been in and around Wilmington, during the whole war and never had a glimpse of the elephant until that night. As that volley went through their ranks, "They ran," said the Colonel, "and I have no doubt they are still running for we were never able to get ten of them together after their flight."

Johnson was gone the next morning. Our cavalry followed to the river, while we took up the line of march for Goldsboro.

CORP. THEODORE D. NEIGHBOR, CO. D.

CHAPTER XVI.

FROM GOLDSBORO—TO THE CLOSE.

WE reached Goldsboro on the 23rd, ragged and shoeless, having been shut up in a hostile country for a little more than two months. Gen. Schofield had entered that place two days before with little or no opposition. Gen. Terry took possession of Cox's Bridge on the Neuse river, ten miles above, on the same day, so that the three armies were in connection, and the great object of the campaign was accomplished. The sea coast was clear from Savannah to Newberne, and our base of supplies secured. We are to rest and refit our army, preparatory to the next move. In less than two weeks thirty thousand were supplied with shoes, and a hundred thousand with clothing.

What a camp we had on all the slopes around Goldsboro. In the solemn forests and spreading fields, the tents of the army were pitched, and the toil-worn veterans took a long holiday. Sherman turned over the army to Schofield, and went to City Point to meet Gen. Grant, where he also met President Lincoln. He was given a royal welcome by both of these great men, and here he arranged to co-operate with Grant in the investment of Richmond.

We were at Goldsboro sixteen days, putting in our time watching a division of colored troops drill in a large, open field near by. The boys who had sworn "they would never fire another gun if the nigger was freed," changed their minds while here, when they heard Terry's men tell the story of the bloody charge of that black division at Ft. Fisher, and here witnessed the steady step and efficient evolutions of battalion drill on the field. They said, "Welcome, my black brother, you are not half so odious as treason and traitors."

It seemed sad that men, who had escaped death in the fury of battle, must be shot down by the enemy, when the advantage was on their side. A number of our pickets were shot while here, by rebel scouts, who would creep up and send a bullet into the body or brain of many a brave man. Quite a number of absentees came up from Kingston. Most of them were men who had been wounded in the Atlanta campaign and had made their way to the east, and down the sea-coast to Kingston, thus increasing our number on dress parade from two hundred and ninety-two, to three hundred and twenty-two.

We began to move on Johnson April 10th. Eleven months before, Sherman had moved on this same Johnson, many hundred miles from here, when hope was mixed with doubt. Now with an army almost the same in numbers, he moves in an opposite direction, believing that the remnant of the army of traitors will be ground to powder between the upper millstone, Grant's army, and the nether millstone, the swift-marching legions of Sherman, aided by an almighty providence, thus destroy the image of iron and brass and clay and scatter it to the four winds. As we advanced he retreated, burning the bridges. We made about twelve miles a day, pressing his rear guard very closely. I think I am right when I say that the last fighting was done by our brigade on the evening of the 12th, when the 22nd Indiana lost quite a number, killed and wounded.

On the evening of the 12th Sherman received a dispatch announcing the surrender of Lee's army, to Grant. The whole army almost went crazy. Joy knew no bounds. It seemed that Pandemonium had broken loose. "Old Billy" was as crazy as any one, for in the height of his joy' he shouted, "Glory to God and our glorious country!" We sang "Coronation," "Praise God From Whom all Blessings Flow," and "John Brown's Body."

The surrender of Lee changed our route materially. The left wing was to go to Smithfield, then out to Warrington; Schofield by Whaley's Mills, and Rolesville. The right wing to Nahunta and from there to Warrington. Now we are ordered to concentrate on Raleigh and from there, south-west to Ashboro, thus preventing any organized forces of Lee's army, that might come south, from escaping into Georgia. Our troops, led by the 9th Ohio cavalry, occupied Raleigh on the 13th, marching in the direction of Durham's station.

Raleigh is the capital of North Carolina, situated in Wake county. It is beautifully located, and had a population of seven thousand when we entered it. Johnson seemed to move rapidly, and indicated a desire to avoid a battle, by turning his course to the south-west. The next day a detail of twenty-five men from the regiment, went out in search of grain and forage for the horses. On our return a body of rebel cavalry charged the rear of the train, capturing Emory Smyth, and William K Shultz of Co. G. The latter was shot down after he had surrendered, and is buried in Raleigh. He was a brave soldier, universally beloved by the members of his company. Johnson proposed an armistice to consider terms of surrender on the evening of the 15th, proposing that hostilities should cease while the matter of the surrender was being considered. Just as Gen. Sherman and his officers were starting for the interview, on the morning of the 17th, he received a dispatch containing the dreadful news of the assassination of President Lincoln. Sherman pledged the operator to the strictest secrecy of the contents of the dispatch, fearing the result of its announcement to the army, while negotiations were pending. The dispatch was promulgated on his return. It spread like wildfire, and we were plunged in a moment from the pinnacle of rejoicing to the lowest depths of grief. To every soldier Lincoln's death came as a sore, personal bereavement.

For a time we were dazed, then the fountains of the great deep were broken up and hundreds of those bronzed veterans wept like children. It was darkness at noontide. Even the people of the south felt that they had lost a friend.

There was little thought of vengeance, but it was almost more than we could bear. Our feelings went out in contempt for the peace at any price sympathizers and rebels of the North who will answer for the death of our Martyred President. Sherman's terms of surrender were disapproved by Hallock, and Grant was sent to Raleigh and directed to proceed with operations against the enemy.

Grant came and quietly sent Sherman to treat with Johnson as though nothing had happened. Johnson came to terms on the 26th of April. Grant read the memorandum of agreement carefully, signed it, and leaving us the next day, took the same to Washington. We knew the war was over and our eyes turned wistfully towards home. We were two hundred and forty miles from Richmond, and expected to reach that place in twenty days. How thankful we were that only one had been killed and five taken prisoner since we left Goldsboro. An order was issued, "That those who were not able for the march, would be sent by way of the coast and up the Atlantic to City Point. Only about two from each company, availed themselves of this offer, preferring the chance of standing the march, and the apportunity of seeing Richmond and the battle fields of the east, to a ride on an ocean vessel, home. We were not long in getting ready.

On the morning of April 30th, stripped of everything but shelter tents, blankets and guns, we started for Richmond. Our cartridge boxes were emptied the first day and the boxes filled with love letters and sacred pictures that we had carried the three years, and such relies from the knapsack as we wanted to preserve. Had the inspector came around he might have taken us for the secretary of war.

We met an occasional squad of Lee's army on their way home, who greeted us with the salutation, "Its all over, and you'uns can have her—what's left of her." Our route was free from swamps, being on the left of the line of march. We crossed the Roanoke river at Clarksville. It was much the widest river we had crossed, since we left home, requiring all the pontoons of the left wing to span it. The Roanoke is formed by the Staunton and Dan rivers, and is navigable for the distance of two hundred and fifty miles. The valley is very fertile and had suffered very little during the war.

After leaving the valley the country was very poor, particularly in Mecklenburg county, where the farms had grown over with stubby pine, leaving the print of the corn rows, when last tilled We were informed one morning that if we expected to see the capital of the defunct confederacy, we would have to scratch gravel, as a race was up between the 14th and 20th corps and our march through the streets of Richmond would depend upon our reaching the James river first. As we crossed the state line into the—"Old Dominion"—Virginia, we thought of the name—how significant. The first of the colonies to swear allegiance to King George the second, and the last to witness the dreadful death gasp of the dying Confederacy. We had marched through every seceding state except Arkansas, Louisiana, Texas and Florida, and the end had come in old Virginia, the "Mother of Presidents."

The signs on the warehouses, "Plaster Mills" and Guano, which were to be seen in every town and cross road, were suggestive that the "sacred soil" needed all sorts of tonics to keep it up. For the sweat of the brow that used to fall there, never yet fattened the ground it fell on. But the fields of the Old Dominion grew richer every day during that conflict, for the rain was red that watered them; but the God of our Fathers cleared away the cloud. We reached the James river May 8th, making an average of twenty-five miles a day. The last day was a race for the goal. Starting at five, we reached Manchester opposite Richmond at seven, making forty-six miles, gaining the race by several hours. Much feeling existed in Sherman's army, on account of the treatment their commander had received at the hands of Secretary Stanton and General Hallock in regard to the terms offered in the surrender of Johnson's army. They had purposely tried to wound and humble him in the very hour of triumph. Gen. Sherman felt deeply wronged, and his men who had marched with him to treasures and triumphs were mad.

How we recall the words of "Uncle Billy" when speaking of those men who slept in comfort and security, while we watched on distant lines. It was cruel to be thus traduced by those whom no motive could induce to shoulder a musket. Our men resented the insult with the approval of the loyal North by marching through the city, and passing Gen. Hallock's headquarters without the usual recognition of rank or command.

Richmond is ninety-five miles south-west of Washington, and had a population of forty thousand when captured. It is a significant fact in history that General Weitzel's brigade of colored troops were the first to enter the city. Many of those black men who marched through it on the day of its capture, April 3d, 1865, had been slaves all their lives until Lincoln's emancipation proclamation was issued.

We saw but little of the city, except the ruin in its evacuation. Four great government warehouses had been fired by General Ewell as his troops marched out. The flames spread from street to street, destroying fully one-third of the city. As we passed Old Libby prison we thought how many brave men had gone in there to come out no more, yet they still live in song and story.

Our route to Washington took us over many of the prominent battle fields of the East. Crossing the Rapidan at Ely's Ford on the evening of the second day, we camped on part of the Wilderness battlefield. The battle lasted three days and was remarkable for many things. Grant had two hundred and fifty pieces of artillery; yet in the main they slept idly in rows under the trees, wholly useless in that struggle. The contending hosts could only see each other as they met face to face. Two of the mightiest armies that ever met on this continent fought hard for three days, yet to us it looked like bushwhacking through a forest eight miles in extent. Grant could not see his army; he could only hear it. The roar and din told of a great conflict. The endurance of the men on both sides was wonderful. Thirty thousand, probably, fell and the victory was Grant's.

How interesting the route became to us. On the same roads on which the armies of the North and South had marched and countermarched, during the past four years of struggle and doubt, but the end had come, and now our army of the West could, unmolested, journey homeward, viewing as we went the scenes and struggles of our comrades in the East. Going up like the children of Israel to rejoice with them in the triumphs of our arms.

Crossing the Rappahannock, a few miles below Fredricksburgh, we soon came in sight of the historic "Mannassas Plains," which was literally covered with fortified lines. At the close of the war farms sold on the plains for ten dollars an acre. Our last camp before reaching Washington was on Bull Run battlefield. What disaster to the Union cause was that Fourth of July battle. Had we routed Beauregard's army, the conflict might have ended before Christmas. On a large beech tree on the bank of the little stream, we noticed the name of W. H. Reynolds, Co. H, 2nd Ohio. As a member of Co. E, 52nd, he was seriously wounded at Kenesaw Mountain, June 27th, 1864, and was discharged for disability from the same. He edited the Ashland Times, and was brutally murdered, while testifying in a court of justice in the peaceful village of Orange, O., October 29th, 1887. A sad ending of a brave manly man.

Light hearted and free, we journey from Bull Run to Arlington, pitching our tents on the Heights early in the afternoon of May the 19th. Right in the rear of our camp, among the trees, lifted the columned front of the Arlington House, the abandoned home of General Robert E. Lee. The property was confiscated by our government and used as a burial place for our "honored dead." The odl mansion-house is used as a place of reception of the thousands of those who visit the capital. The National Cemetery on the Heights is filled with the dead from the battle fields of the army of the Potomac.

It seemed almost like a dream to us, as we sat in front of our tents, gazing upon the scene before us. Our long march is ended. We had crossed and recrossed eight states, traveling, on foot and by rail, nearly eight thousand miles. Our arms have been victorious, our country saved, and we are to join the nation, now assembling at her capital, in celebrating the victory.

Just across the Potomac was the dome of the capitol. Like Lookout Mountain, at Chattanooga, you can never lose sight of it. White tents could be seen everywhere, for the greatest army of the nineteenth century had gathered

JAMES M. KNISELY, DRUM MAJOR

here. Down the Potomac were forts and defenses. But the scene on the river made you forget its shores. Boats coming and going, with sails like a cloud above a cloud, every one of them dotted with soldier boys. But they were all alike in one thing: they all carried the flag of victory, vast and broad, flopping like an eagle's wings, just as we had seen it on the field of battle. Washington's defenses were immense. Sixty forts filled with sixty batteries, ribbed with rifle pits, loaded with bombs; all woven in the loom of war.

The crowd was immense. More than 200,000 soldiers. And a hundred thousand citizens of the great North, were humming round the hotels or on the streets, while the newsboys were crying, "All about the parade." Gladness beamed from their faces everywhere. There were recognitions that made everybody glad. Two brothers, lost to each other for years, one was with Grant, the other with Lee, met here face to face and knew each other.

Grant's army was reviewed on the 23rd. The day was delightful and the parade was imposing. Part of Sherman's army crossed the Potomac in the evening of the 23rd and bivouaced in the streets around the capitol, while the 14th Corps moved down to the "Long Bridge" and camped for the night.

We had spent the 23rd in brightening up our guns and mountings, and getting our soiled clothing in the best condition, that we might be ready to keep step on the morrow. As we crossed the bridge the next morning, command was given to break step and march in open order that a swinging motion might be avoided; the bridge being considered unsafe.

At nine o'clock the Signal gun was fired. Sherman and Howard rode slowly up Pennsylvania avenue, accompanied by their staff officers. We wondered, as the column started, why General Logan was in command of the army of the Tennessee, while Gen. Howard, who had commanded it after

Gen. McPherson's death, was with Sherman at the head of the procession. Gen. Howard, in his Memoirs, tells us that "it was the highest ambition of his life to march that day with the men who had helped to make him what he was." When General Sherman said to him, "You will march at the head of the right wing," he resented the proposal with emphasis. General Sherman said to him calmly: "Howard you are a Christian. Suffer it to be so for my sake." and the Christian soldier submitted without a murmur.

The western army was six hours in passing the reviewing stand in the following order, fifteenth, seventeenth, and fourteenth corps, sixty-five thousand men of splendid physique, who had marched nearly one thousand miles through a hostile country. Now they are almost at the end of the stadium on which hangs an immortal crown, while a great cloud of witnesses are watching. Our own loyal-hearted, liberty-loving people to applaud and approve, while foreigners looked on and were amazed. Many good people had looked upon our western army as a sort of a mob, but they were compelled to admit its superior organization and discipline.

Pap Thomas' old corps, the fourteenth, commanded by General Jeff C. Davis was the last to pass the reviewing stand, followed by the train of foragers, with pack mules carrying poultry, hams, and all kinds of Southern food for man and beast. In the procession were milch cows, goats, and army pets. Last of all came the "redeemed of the Lord," with songs and everlasting joy upon their heads. They came in whole families, shouting as they led the children, saying, "Glory to God and Massa Sherman."

The minister from the court of Germany became greatly interested in the scene, as the 15th and 17th corps passed with steady step and perfect demeanor, he said to Bishop Ames, who sat by him on the reviewing stand, bishop, "An army like that could whip all Europe." As the 20th corps passed he said excitedly, bishop, "An army like that could whip the world." When the 14th had passed with the train of foragers, slapping the bishop on the shoulder, he shouted, "An army like that could whip the devil."

The *crowning* day is over and the sun had burned its way into the afternoon as we stacked arms near the Old Soldier's Home, north of the capitol. Here we put up our tents awaiting the final march—"The home stretch." Two weeks passed very pleasantly in eating and sleeping and sight-seeing in the city, with an occasional guard duty. The Christian commission generously donated a supply of pickled onions and canned goods, of which they seemed to have a surplus when the war closed. Squads of four were permitted to stroll in the park or go through the Capitol, with its stately columns. Or by the Treasury, where our "Greenbacks" were to come from. Or on the grounds where we might view the uncertain magnificence of the President's mansion.

All these had a new meaning to us. Had the Union been rent these doubtless would have fallen to the enemy, but now they are ours. Hancock's veteran corps, the 2nd, made up of veterans who had re-enlisted for the war, were on guard in the city. Their dress suits were new and of a light blue color, braided, and were handsome, making quite a contrast with the faded blouse of the army of the west. Everything went smoothly until the question of merit and superiority came up, when one of our boys shouted, "Bull Run," quick as lightning came the retort, "Chickamauga." The discussion ended good naturedly in the exultation chorused by all, "We whipped them anyway, didn't we."

When Sunday came, we put on our best, and like the ship's crew when the captain ordered them aloft, we polished our buttons. On the streets we were impressed with the change of the African in habits and dress. The old mantle of the aristocracy of the South seemed to fall upon the ex-slave. *He* sported his best, swung his cane, pulled his hat over his eyebrow and gave the old plantation laugh. *She* was out, flounced, laced and beautified.

The story of the war contains abundant proof that our black brother did possess a nobler quality than mere animal courage. That he did touch the heroic height that makes life grand, and death a poem. That black color bearer, who planted the flag on the enemy's works at Fort Fisher, who when shot down crept away, bleeding and faint, still bearing the flag aloft said, as he sank down, "I never let it touch the ground." That man has at least one foot on the pedestal where stands the white hero of the superior race.

The mustering officer came June 3rd and mustered us out of the volunteer service. Acting Mustering Officer Lieutenant George Scroggs, of the 125th Illinois of our own brigade, being assigned to that duty. His autograph at the bottom of a little piece of parchment was more valuable than any 160 acres of land, because it had the word *Honorable* on it—is known and read by every boy that received it, for its boldness. It does seem sometimes that he wrote it with a bayonet, but it is none the less valuable to us.

Of the ten hundred and ninety-two enlisted men borne upon the muster rolls, three hundred and forty-five were mustered out with the regiment. A number of these met us from detail service at Camp Chase for final discharge. Of the Field and Staff Officers, who were mustered when the regiment was organized, not one of them were at the final muster out.

Of the line officers who held commissions at Camp Dennison, the following came home with us: Captain Charles W. Clancy, Co. B, promoted to colonel. Captain J. Taylor Holmes, Co. G, promoted to lieutenant colonel. First Lieutenants W. H. Bucke, Co. A, Abisha C. Thomas, Co. C, and Samuel C. Hutchinson, Co. F, were promoted to captains of their respective companies and mustered out with them. Second Lieutenants W. A. Judkins, Co. B, and S. J. Brent, Co. K, were promoted to first lieutenants, but were on detached duty most of the time, and were mustered out with the regiment. Two officers, Colonels Clancy and Holmes, were prisoners.

How we regretted to part from the other regiments of the third brigade. The farewell must be final. We had marched and camped and fought together, for more than a thousand days. Our interests had become mutual and we loved each other as brothers. No jealousies had ever estranged us. And we are certain no better material went to the war from the states of Illinois and Indiana than the three regiments from the "Prairie State" and the one from the "Hoosier State," who with our regiment were known as Dan McCook's Brigade of the Fourteenth Corps. These men have nothing but praise for Colonel McCook and his *own* regiment, the 52nd Ohio. More than half of the brigade have died since the war, but we hope to meet the remnant in a brigade reunion in the near future.

June the 7th orders came to be ready to move toward the Setting Sun—we are "going home to die no more"—by the cruel hand of war. We had a wait at the Baltimore and Ohio depot of five hours. Half the sympathy we had bottled up and corked for the government for its delays had evaporated by the time our train came. But it came, not the cozy high top passenger coach like that we rode in to Camp Dennison, but a train of box cars which recalled to mind the boy's prophesy, "When we come back they will let us ride in cattle cars." We were loaded in box cars, labeled "Merchandise"—precious freight; forty men in a car. We thought it only for a night or two, thinking that joy cometh in the morning.

Morning came and we had not made a hundred miles· Noon came and we were at Point of Rocks. Night came and we pulled into Cumberland, Md., with a promise of supper. All we got was a tin of coffee. Erecting our tent on the top of a flat car and tying a rope around our bodies, fastening one end to the foot-pad. Col. Clancy and I went supperless to bed. Slowly our train crept up the mountain, and just as the morning walked to and fro upon the top of night we woke. Looking down from that mountain top we did not wonder that God gave The Law from Sinai, or that the beatitudes were shed like Herman's dew, from a mountain.

At last we came to the foot and to broader ground, where the valley of the Ohio bears us company. Up the river we slowly traveled, arriving at Bellaire in the evening. The last view we had of the Ohio and our native state was at Covington, Kentucky, in August, '62.

Crossing over on ferry boats in the evening, we tarried all night on board the cars. Early in the morning of the fourth day we started for Columbus. As the day dawned clear, we thought we could breathe more freely and purely, as we were now in God's country, passing within a few miles of the old home we cherished in our boyhood, as we neared Cambridge. Visions of breakfast prepared by mother's hands flashed before me, but it soon vanished. Nearing Zanesville the boys determined to make a raid on the stores for something to eat, when officers discovered the plot and our train ran through the city, stopping at the shops just outside the city of Newark, where we were side-tracked and a guard thrown around us, no one being allowed to leave the car.

Soon a crowd of women and boys were tempting us with baskets filled with good things, while not a greenback could be found in the company or regiment. While discussing whether there would be greater honor in suffering the pangs of hunger, than to justify what our consciences knew to be wrong by urging the necessities of the case, a well dressed young man crossed the track and enquired, "What regiment is this?" We told him, and he said, "Colonel Dan McCook's old regiment, you never need be ashamed of *your* record." We spoke of our trip home and of hunger. When he purchased every basket with their contents from the venders, paying their price, and set them in the car. I have always regretted that, while every man was, like the prophet's servant, "busy here and there, the man was gone." While each one was looking after his share of the generous and timely gift, the young man with the silk hat and kid gloves slipped away and we never knew who our benefactor was. But away down in our heart of hearts we have deposited a share of gratitude for our young friend and cultured gentleman, who had a heart in him as big as a meeting house.

Arriving at Columbus, we went across to Todd's Barracks and sat down to a dinner, furnished by our friends in the city. Governor Brough and others welcomed us back in patriotic eloquence.

Every man was happy in the thought that we would have a refreshing sleep, that would be unbroken by war's alarms, or the rattle of the train. But, alas, there was a night attack. An army of bed bugs, famous for their size, followed by battalion after battalion of grey backs, whose stomachs were as voracious as the men's who stood around the tables that afternoon after a two days' fast.

We pitched our tents in Camp Chase the next day to await the coming of the man with the iron box.

There were about six thousand soldiers who were waiting for a chance to go home. Three fragments of regiments, including our own, were the only organized troops there. The rest were from the prisons of the South, waiting to be mustered ont. These men became restless and complained of the delay. Many of them were weak and anxious to get where some one would share with them in their sufferings. Many had sent home for money, with which they could buy delicacies and things they had longed for.

The sutlers inside the grounds were selling these much higher than they could be bought outside. A report had been in circulation that the commander, Gen. Buckingham, had an interest in these stores. A few nights after we arrived, there was a noiseless tread about, 10 o'clock. A shot, a crash, and the stores were overturned. A soldier was shot, a sutler missing, and never more heard of, the goods were carried away, and not a vestige of them could be found the next morning.

Fortunately the three regiments had not turned over their arms and the threatening danger from the six thousand rebel prisoners in the stockade was averted by doubling the guards. But these excited and restless men continued to avenge themselves by tearing down the high fence on the west and south, thus, by the bonfire made, they not only consumed the lumber, but consigned to the flames the goods they had taken from the sutler's stores. A regiment of troops from camp Dennison arrived at daylight to find all things quiet.

The paymaster came Saturday with deed in hand, signed and sealed, which was to be our passport to a civillian's rights of citizenship—an honorable discharge. Before payment, he informed the officers and men that the government had generously deducted nine dollars and forty-five cents from each man's pay to reimburse the government and sutlers for the property taken and destroyed by the raiders. The officers and men were indignant. But few of our men participated in the raid, although the whole regiment was in sympathy with the men who had been shamefully mistreated while here in camp as well as in Andersonville.

The remonstrance against the reduction was long and loud, the men refusing to touch the money. Late in the afternoon a dispatch came from Edward M. Stanton, secretary of war, who had been appealed to early in the morning, ordering the full payment of all dues.

Each man answered to his name, received his wages for services rendered and one hundred dollars government bounty, pledged to the army by act of Congress, and an Honorable Discharge. Adieus were spoken and the 52nd was borne away to their homes.

It was good bye comrades, good bye officers, good bye blankets, haversacks and canteens. Good bye dear old shelter tent. I shall sleep on a bed and eat cooked victuals and live in a house. And now as we live, who are left, and have memories for those who have died and are now encamped "beyond," let us, as we continue our march towards that glorious sunset, keep our eye on the old flag, and as we grow older may we be permitted to encamp in the valley awhile for rest, there to listen for

TAPS.

FIRST LIEUT. CHRISTOPHER W. GRIMES, CO. C.

CHAPTER XVII.

52nd O. V. I. ASSOCIATION.

THE first annual reunion was held in New Comerstown, Ohio, August 26th, 1875, at which sixty-one members were present. Steps were taken for the organization of an association for the purp ise of holding an annual reunion and taking such action from time to time as may seem proper in the interest of the survivors of the regiment, or the families of deceased comrades The organization was completed at the reunion held the following year in Steubenville, Ohio, December 25th, 1876, which made all who served in the regiment eligible to membership in the association, and the widows of deceased comrades honorary members, their names to be recorded when reported.

Twenty-four annual meetings have been held. Average attendance about fifty-eight. About three hundred members of the regiment have died since its organization. Captain Samuel Rothacker, was the first president, and S. L. Brice, secretary. The annual gatherings are growing in interest. Let us keep in touch, comrades! J. B. Work, Co. G. Room 205, Cook County Court House, Chicago, Ill., is the present president, and N. B. Stewart, Claysville, Ohio, secretary.

CHAPTER XVIII.

ASSOCIATION OF THE SONS AND DAUGHTERS OF THE REGIMENT.

THIS association effected an organization at Barnesville, Ohio, September 22nd, 1899, presenting the following constitution, which was adopted, and approved by the regimental Association.

1st. This organization shall be known as the Sons and Daughters of the 52nd O. V. I. Association.

2nd. The object of this association is to perpetuate and keep fresh in the memories of the children of the men who enlisted in the 52nd regiment, the service and deeds of valor of all honorably discharged members of said regiment and of those who gave their lives in the war of the Rebellion.

3rd. Its membership shall consist of the sons and daughters of all honorably discharged soldiers of the 52nd O. V. I. There shall be no limit to age.

4th. All applications for membership shall be made to the secretary of this association, who shall ascertain from the secretary of the 52nd O. V. I. Association as to eligibility to membership.

5th. The officers of this association shall consist of a president, vice-president, secretary and treasurer. The office of secretary and treasurer may be combined. The president shall preside at all meetings and perform such duties as are prescribed by the rules governing the office of President of the Regimental Association.

In like manner all other offices of the association shall be filled. The offices vacant shall be filled by the members present.

6th. The meetings of this association shall be held upon the same date as the annual reunion of the regiment and at the same place, and shall be governed, and its records approved, by the regimental association before such records shall be made official.

7th. The officers shall be elected annually and hold their offices until their successors are elected and notice of their acceptance given the Regimental secretary of the association.

This constitution shall go into effect when approved by both organizations.

Let all comrades send the names of their children to the secretary for enrollment.

L. Ruth Work,
Mrs. Mame Porter,
Charles E. Stewart,
Committee.

THE ORGANIZATION.

COMPANY A.

COMPANY A was from Van Wert and Paulding counties. Capt. Clark was from Van Wert city, where he died in 1883. Lieut. Bucke was from Dayton, and now lives at 304 Fourth avenue, New York. He was mustered out as Captain. The whereabouts of Lieuts. Kaufman and Dunham are unknown. Lieut. Lane was mustered out with Co. E. Lieut. Adam Knecht was on detached duty, and died in Dayton in 1892. The Company mustered ninety-three men. They were excellent fighters and always did good work on the skirmish line. Nineteen of the company were killed or wounded, and thirty-four were mustered out with the regiment. We have kept in touch with the living, and they often speak of their brave men, who fell, on the Atlanta campaign, and of the living, who are honored citizens, we know the Scott brothers, the Baxters, Frank Leslie and John I. Cable, of Van Wert, O., Corporal James Conway, of Mechanicsburg, O., who always suggests a prayer for Col. Dan McCook's soul when he sends his annual greeting to the boys. S. B. Marshall died in Agosta, a few years ago, where he was located in the practice of medicine. A number of the company cannot be located, they are "Only remembered for what they have done."

COMPANY B.

Company B was recruited in Smithfield and Mt. Pleasant, in Jefferson county, with just one hundred and three men. Dr. C. W. Clancy was the captain. He was twenty-nine years old, as brave and true a man as ever drew a sword. He was succeeded in command of the company by Captain Sturgis, who was wounded at Resaca, and discharged in August on account of the disability incurred. The Captain lives near California, Mo. Lieut. W. A Judkins was on detached duty as a member of Gen. Mason's staff. He shares the confidence of the citizens of Smithfield, as he grows older in the honorous duties of church and state. The Company was originally recruited for the 98th Ohio. Seventy-one were from Smithfield and thirty-two from Mt. Pleasant. They reported to Col. Webster at Mingo, and found Col. Dan McCook there with an order for the transfer to the 52nd Ohio. They were a fine looking set of men, not a man under eighteen, or over forty-five, the average being twenty-four and a fraction. Twenty-four of the company are buried in the South, and thirty-eight were mustered out with the regiment. Samuel Grimshaw wears a medal from the government for bravery at Kenesaw. Of the dead, they were the bravest and the best. Of the living, year by year they grow dearer to us, for the ties were welded in the fires of battle. There were the Flemming's and Mercer's and Kirk's and Harrison's. J. C. was the first to enlist in the company, and got an empty sleeve at "Buzzard's Glory," and has found favor at home, having served twenty-one years as postmaster. Towering among the boys of the Company was good-natured Jim McDonald. But I must not dwell, I am only to confess and not boast.

COMPANY C.

Company C was recruited in Belmont county, Barnesville, Somerton and Boston furnishing most of the men. Dr. Moffitt, Captain; Abisha C. Thomas, First Lieutenant and E. E. Mills, Second Lieutenant. Dr. Moffitt resigned at Nashville, and Captain Thomas was at the head of the Company and in the thickest of the fight, while the war lasted, and not a hair of his head was touched, and he still lives honored and beloved by every surviving member of the regiment.

The Company mustered eighty-nine men, average age, twenty-six; oldest, fifty-one; youngest, sixteen. Of the Company that fell on bloody Kenesaw, most of them were color guards. Will Bradfield, Fenton Carter and Linley Street were around the old flag until it reached the hill top. Twenty-nine of the Company were killed or wounded. Few of them died in the hospital, indicating that they came from the headwaters of "Captina." They were brave and good men, deserving the honors they won. Christopher W. Grimes rose from the ranks to Brevet Captain. He lives near New Matamoras, O. For twenty years he cared for his aged mother, her afflictions affecting both body and mind, requiring his constant care, for which he deserves great honor.

Captain Grimes, who with the Company, marched and fought to Atlanta and to the sea, speaks of those who died, as living, because they died that the nation might live. The Captain draws upon his recollection of the men, as they one by one pass before him. He speaks of Thomas, who never was gloomy, in the darkest hour brave and loyal was he. Of Starbuck, the hero of Bentonville. He takes us back to the campfire, and fancies he hears "Flick" Hunt cussing and discussing the same subject, a Hunt that was always ready to hunt the enemy. And the "six-footer," patient Billy

Carter, who always had tobacco. And the small and neat Fenton Carter, who fell at Resaca, and sleeps now at Chattanooga. Of James Lynne, wounded on the enemy's works at Kenesaw, now living at Cumberland, O. But we cannot speak personally of all. However, I must tell you that the Captain writes words of love and friendship, thanking all for what they did for him and their country, hoping all who are living may "fight the good fight of faith" and be ready for the last roll call.

COMPANY D.

Company D was from Tuscarawas county, New Philadelphia and New Comerstown furnishing most of the men. It mustered one hundred and five and was officered by Captain M. L. Morrow, 1st Lieut. John H. Collier, 2nd Lieut. S. M. Neighbor. Capt. Morrow received his commission as Major to date from March 8, 1863, but Col. McCook did not like him and ordered the adjutant to give no papers that would enable him to be mustered. When the field and staff muster rolls were ready to sign, the Captain signed his name as Major Commanding instead of Captain Commanding. He was a splendid penman and with a flourish wrote the word Major over the word Captain. The rolls were sent to Brigade headquarters and in ten minutes Colonel McCook was on his way to Nashville, to telegraph to Gov. Todd. A commission came for Capt. Holmes, and he was mustered as Major, Morrow resigned, and in a short time was made a Major in in the pay master's department, thus securing one of the best positions in the army.

But the regiment secured a man as Major who was honored by every man in the regiment. Morrow died shortly after the war. Lieut. Collier resigned July 29, 1863, and lived to be an old man, dying in Topeka, Kansas, in 1899, aged 81.

Lieut. Neighbor was promoted to Captain and fell at Kenesaw, mortally wounded, dying in Chattanooga, July 7, 1864. Capt. Neighbor was a brave and efficient officer, beloved by his men and fellow officers. He never failed or faltered in duty. A few of his men could not write and he did not like marks on the pay roll. These men were instructed by the Captain at his tent, until most of them could write to friends at home. In all their needs he was a friend and counselor. Up to the slope of the mountain he led his company that morning at Kenesaw. When near the summit he sank with his dead and dying comrades, his right lung pierced by a bullet—his life work done, his mission and calling fulfilled. His brother, David Neighbor, who was commissioned 2nd Lieut. in 1863, had his right leg crushed in a collision on the railway at La Vergne, Tennessee. He was totally disabled for the service and was discharged. When Captain Neighbor fell, the command of the company rested on 1st. Sergeant William P. Mulvane. Until the close of that campaign, "Finn," as he is called, was an excellent soldier. He is an honored citizen of New Comerssown, Ohio, at the present time. He resists the encroachments of old age,—is surrounded with the good things of this life, still keeping in touch with his comrades, who followed, with him, the old flag.

Capt. James M. Summers, promoted from Company H, took command of Company D at Savannah. He was popular with his company, a good soldier, and gave his life fighting for the old flag at Averysboro, on March 16, 1865. His wound was almost similar to the fatal wound of Captain Neighbor. He is buried at Newberne, N. C.

The command fell upon First Lieut. W. H. Ray, who was mustered out with the company. "Harvey" still lives and has spent the years since the close of the war as Superintendent of the public schools at Uhrichsville, New Philadelphia, and Carrollton, Ohio, where he now lives and fills the position.

Company D lost more men than any company in the regiment. Nineteen were killed or died from wounds, twenty-six were wounded, fourteen died of disease in the hospital, and thirty-four were mustered out with the company. The company is before me today, and most of their faces are familiar. There is Lowmiller, who was a recruit, and fell at Dallas. There is Johnny Sill, how his poor mother used to come to our reunions, while she lived, and listen to stories of her brave boy's death, as he went up Kenesaw, hat in one hand, and gun in the other. And I see poor Francis Grace, who fell on the breast works, and James Beard, so young and loyal. Then Armstrong and Daugherty and Shackle, all of whom lay in the sun that afternoon mortally wounded. I then turn to the living, whose foreheads are wrinkled and locks are gray. There are the two Neighbor boys, George and Theodore. George was a priosner at Peach Tree, and in Andersonville six months, and "Dode," as we called him, came out with as vivid a recollection of what he saw, as any man in the army. He is a well-to do merchant of New Comerstown, O. He never misses a reunion. He has two excellent qualities, he loves home, has an excellent family, and he loves the boys who saved our country. Jehu Peck came home, settled down as a shoe merchant in New Comerstown, Ohio, and is a clean, christian gentleman, the kind of a man that makes a good citizen. There is Gilbert L. Patterson, with the best of a record as a soldier and citizen, as well. And John Smith, a cheerful, whole-souled companion, who, because of his smooth, boyish face, was known as "Kate." There was John Kirk with his big knapsack, and Anthony Hartley the great forager. The rebs captured him at Fenn's bridge, loaded with chickens and forage of all kinds. I re-

LIEUT. ALEXANDER B. McINTYRE, CO. E.

fer with pride to the record of Sergeant John W. Baltzley, so brave, he lay against the earthworks at Kenesaw, when they pulled him over, and he was a prisoner until the close of the war. He lived and died in Zanesville, Ohio. Thirty-three have died since the war.

COMPANY E.

Company E was recruited by three men, Parker A. Elson at Steubenville, Alexander Smith at New Alexandria and H. O. Mansfield at Bloomfield in Jefferson county. We had one hundred and six men. The average age of these men was twenty-three. The oldest man enlisted was Harmon Hukill. He is now living near Claysville, Ohio, at the advanced age of 84 years. The youngest, Frank Carnahan, is fifty-three. The company had thirteen killed and thirty-four wounded. Thirty-eight have died since the war. Captain Elson was a jolly good fellow. He was in California six years, came home and worked as a contractor and builder. He died in Steubenville in 1886 at the age of sixty-one.

Lieut. Alexander Smith resigned and came home in January '63. He was Captain in the one-hundred day service, and was elected Sheriff of Jefferson county, serving two terms. He died in New Alexandria in August 1897.

Henry O. Mansfield recruited about thirty men and there was a contest between he and Patrick Shannon of Steubenville for 2nd Lieut. It was left to the company to elect and Mansfield was elected and commissioned. He was promoted to Captain after the battle of Stone river and led the company until he was wounded in the charge at Kenesaw, which disabled him for further service. He settled in Scio, O., was respected and honored by all who knew him. His service, which continued almost two years, was honorable and he had the confidence of his men. He died in 1896, aged sixty-two.

Lieut. James H. Donaldson commanded the company from Kenesaw to Peach Tree creek, where he fell to rise no more. His body was removed to Steubenville, O., where it lies in the soldiers' lot.

Sergeant E. T. Hanlon took command at Peach Tree and continued with the company until Sherman left for the sea-coast. Lieut. A. B. McIntyre led the company to Savannah, where W. H. Lane was promoted from 1st Lieut of Co. A, to Captain and transferred to our company. The Captain was wounded at Peach Tree. He was highly respected by all the members of the Company. He won the hearts of the men by his courage and kindness. He came to the regiment from Chicago, enlisted in Co. A as a private. carried a gun, and by his bravery and excellent character, rose from the ranks to Captain, on his own merits. He was mustered out with the company and lives at Bellfontaine, O.

We were proud of the company while in the service and have reason to know that they have been the same loyal citizens of this great country. Many of them have filled positions of honor, and credit to themselves. Lieut. McIntyre has filled the office of Sheriff of Morgan county, Lieut. Smith of Jefferson county, A. C. Blackburn Auditor of Jefferson county and John C. Brown was three times elected treasurer of Jefferson county and three times treasurer of the state of Ohio.

Seventy out of the one-hundred and eighteen enlisted men are dead. The forty-eight living can truly say, "They have kept the faith," and await the crowning day. Every comrade in the company is worthy of special mention, but we cannot encroach upon the space allotted in this small volume. Yet every comrade, like the Master, took his special friends up into the mountain apart, so we cannot refrain from mentioning those in whom we especially confided.

There was "Joe" Thompson, twice severely wounded. We fell together and alone on the picket line. We have ever felt as brothers. He is still living near Steubenville, O. We entered the ministry in 1868, and for thirty-two years have watched with great interest the lives of these men. Tommy Thompson, the Mansfield and Moore brothers, David M. Scott, who lost an arm, and Geo. W. Chalfant, who left a leg at bloody Peach Tree, B. H. Maxwell, and a score of others whose army record is of the highest character.

COMPANY F.

Company F was recruited in Belmont county and mustered ninety-eight men. The average age was twenty-seven. Captain Donaldson and 1st Lieut. Irwin resigned in the spring of sixty-three, and Captain Samuel C. Hutchinson commanded the company to the end. The company were efficient skirmishers and did most of the skirmishing for the brigade. Their loss was twenty-three killed and wounded. Captain Hutchinson lives near Milan, Sullivan county, Mo., and has served as sheriff and treasurer of his county. Captain S. L. Brice was promoted from Corporal to 1st Lieut. of his company and served as Quartermaster and Adjutant with great acceptability. He is on the Editorial staff of the Wheeling Register, and has served four years as city solicitor.

Julius Armstrong was promoted to 1st Lieut. and commanded Company H at the close of the war. He now resides in Columbus, O. All of the men of the company who saw service deserve personal mention. There was the Hammond's, Gillespie's, Gates and Vandyne brothers, and Doty's, all good soldiers, and among the many who followed the old flag through to the end and came home with it, was Peter Giffin, who still lives in Flushing, O., to help keep the camp fires burning, and by his honesty and upright life to bless any community in which he may reside.

COMPANY G.

Company G was recruited in Jefferson county, with one hundred men and three officers. The company received eight recruits while in the service. Thirty-eight are living, and seventy-four are dead. Twenty-eight were students in Richmond College. One of the comrades of that company writes me that "the men were above the average intellectually. Of those who came home, those who abused themselves by drink and lived recklessly, are all dead but one." The writer is personally acquainted with nearly all of the survivors, and knows they are men of excellent character. Captain Rothacker still lives in Richmond, O., and has an extensive practice as a physician. He has recently passed through a great trial in the death of his son, John D. Rothacker, who was accidentally killed. The Captain was a brave soldier, and beloved by his men. He had a dread of being wounded and sent to the hospital, and made arrangements, if such a thing occurred, to be cared for by the surgeon of the regiment in the field Lieut. Addison M. Marsh resigned in 1863 He was a printer by trade, and died in New Philadelphia, O., in 1892 at the age of 52. Second Lieut. David F. Miser was wounded at Kenesaw, and died on Lookout Mountain nineteen days after the battle. Lemuel W. Duff was promoted from Company B, and commanded the company through the march northward from Savannah.

Men of note in Church and State came from this company. A. R. Holmes has been Auditor of Tuscarawas county, and has held the office of U. S. Postoffice Inspector continuously for the last fourteen years. T. H. Montgomery has been Sheriff of Jefferson county and is a prosperous business man of Toronto, O. Andrew M. Stevenson has been Superintendent of the Wheeling public schools for almost thirty years. J. B. Work is in Chicago in one of the Cook county offices, where he has held a position for years.

Montgomery was the tallest man, Rhinehart the best forager, Gosset the tailor, Joe Swan the blacksmith. Joe died in Victor, Colorado, in April, 1900. Copeland, the man with the long whiskers, reaching down to his waist. The company had 29 killed and wounded, and made an excellent record in rank and file.

COMPANY H.

Company H. was recruited mostly in Cincinnati. A number of recruits came from Fairfield county. Captain Culbertson served four months, resigned, and died since the war closed. Captain Charles Swift served on Brigade staff, resigned in April, 1865, and died in Cincinnati. Lieut James M. Summers was promoted to Captain of Co. D. Julius Armstrong, First Lieut. of Company F, commanded the company through Sherman's march, and was mustered out with the company. Gossler Rudolf was mustered out as First Sergt., and lives in Cincinnati. "Lud" Mills was noted as the jolly laugher of the regiment. Samuel A. Harper lives at Elmwood, Ill. He has filled the office of Department Commander of the G. A. R. in his state, and is a prosperous man of his city. James C. Michie was commissioned as Captain in the Regular Army, returned home, and has been Quartermaster of the Dayton Soldiers' Home for a number of years. We have not been able to find the men of Co. H since the war. Only nine of the company are known to the writer to be living.

COMPANY I.

Company I was recruited principally in Cleveland, Painesville and the Western Reserve, and mustered ninety-two men, with three recruits. Only nine of the company are known certain to be living. Capt. P. C. Schneider fell at Peach Tree and is buried in Cleveland. He was a brave soldier. Frank B. James was promoted to Captain from Co. K, and commanded the company until mustered out. He enlisted as a private in Co. K and was commissioned as Lieut. in 1863 and Captain in 1864, and to brevet major when mustered out.

The Capt. served in an expedition from Cincinnati to build the Paducah bridge, and was captured at the fight at Cynthiana and escaped. The members of Co. I speak in the highest terms of his bravery and efficiency as a commanding officer. He lives in Cincinnati.

Lieut. George A. Masury served on the Colonel's staff. Lieut Ira H. Pool was an M. E. minister of the Central Ohio Conference, having been in the ministry two years. He was a brave officer. Was mortally wounded at Kenesaw and died July 30th and is buried at Chattanooga.

Lieut. Edwin T. Donaldson was discharged after the battle of Perryville for disability and is an honored citizen of Painesville, O. 1st Sergeant Howell B. Treat came home with the company and is an honored citizen of Painesville. He wears a medal for bravery at Kenesaw.

Albert Button has served two terms as sheriff of Lake county, O., and lives in Painesville. Newton H. Bostwick, whose bravery and capture is narrated in the history of Kenesaw, lives in Chardon, O.

The company lost 34 in killed and wounded and bore a conspicuous part in the regiment's history.

COMPANY K.

Company K was recruited in Cincinnati with quite a number of men from the river towns near the city. Only seven of the company are known to the writer to be living. The company was so reduced at the review at Washington that it marched with Co E The loss in killed and wounded was thirty-one out of 96 men in the start. Capt Bloom served four months, resigned and is still living, an inmate of the Dayton Soldiers' Home. Capt. Ed. L. Anderson was a member of McCook's staff, was mustered out with the company and lives in Cincinnati. The Captain is an artist of note and has spent a good part of his time in Europe. Lieut. Samuel J. Brent was on detached duty most of the time, but was mustered out with the company. He has served as Auditor of Knox county and is located in business in Columbus, O.

Horace B. Church served in the Company until the war closed, enlisted in the Regular Army, had both feet frozen on the plains and they were amputated. He died suddenly in Granville, O , June 5, 1900. Henry Koch was wounded at Kenesaw, and is ending his days in the State Soldiers' Home at Sandusky. "Jack" Jeffers lives at Steese, O. He He was a terror to the officers, also to the rebels. He was in every battle of the regiment and came out without a scratch The company did excellent service, winning laurels in every battle for the Union.

Thirty-two members of the Regiment have been admitted to the Dayton Home. Of that number fourteen have died. There were eight in the Home April 1st, 1900.

The following have died in the State Soldiers' Home, Erie county, O., Richard Blodgett, Co. I, Lieut. Add M Marsh, Co. G, and Fred Siebert, Co. I. Admitted and discharged, John Barkheimer, Co. B, Edward Conley, Co, H, Samuel

Hardy, Co. H, David A. Roe, Co. A, and Byron Smith, Co. K. Present in the Home, May 1st, 1900, George Davis, Co. E, Stewart Doty, Co. F, and Henry Koch, Co. K.

As mustered we had nine hundred and eighty-one men, fourteen Field and Staff Officers, and thirty line officers, these, with the recruits, make a total of 1104. Fourteen were commissioned by promotion from the ranks. Of the fifty-five commissioned officers, thirty five resigned, eight were killed or died of wounds, three were disabled by wounds and discharged, eighteen were wounded and returned to the Regiment. Not one of the fifty-five officers died of disease while in the service. Assistant Surgeon A. J. Rosa died from an overdose of morphine.

SERGT. DAVID M. SCOTT, CO. E.

ROSTER

OF THE

FIFTY-SECOND O. V. I.

IN preparing the roster for this volume, with the limited space at my command, I shall be compelled to abandon the usual method of Company record, and condense as to service, a classified arrangement by companies, and, if possible, account for every name found upon the rolls. To make a perfect roster would be a manifest impossibility. There will be mistakes and omissions, for which no person can be blamed. And to those who survive, we submit the result of our labor, and await your verdict.

FIELD AND STAFF.

Colonel Daniel McCook entered the service as a captain of the shield guards, a part of the First Kansas Regiment, and served under General Lyon at Wilson's Creek. Was chief of staff of the First Division of the army of the Ohio at Shiloh, and received his commission as Colonel of the 52nd Ohio, July 15th, 1862. He was mortally wounded June 27th, 1864, in the assault on Kenesaw Mountain, Ga., and died at Steubenville, O., July 17th, 1864 and was buried at Spring Grove Cemetery, Cincinnatti, O. He was the sixth son of a family of nine boys, and was born in Carrollton, O., in 1834. The father and eight sons were soldiers in the Civil War. All did valiant service for their couutry. Our brave Colonel Dan was promoted to the rank of Brigadier

General, an honor which he refused to accept the day before his death. Colonel McCook read law with Clarence M. Seward, and was at one time a law partner of Edward M. Stanton He was proud of his regiment, also of the number of the regiment. He often referred to the History of the 52nd, an English regiment, which fought from Hindoostan to Waterloo, and would say to the boys, "Let us keep up the record." With tears and wreaths for our brave Dan, who is in the eternal bivouac, we wait to join him at the trumpet call.

Col. John J. McCook, the youngest of Colonel Dan's brothers, enlisted at the age of seventeen in the 6th Ohio Cavalry, was promoted to First Lieutenant, and was with us as a member of General Crittenden's staff at Perryville. He served in Gen. Grant's campaign in the east, and was dangerously wounded at Shady Grove, Va. He was pro_ moted to Lieutenant Colonel for meritorious conduct, and still survives. He and his brother, Gen. A. McDowell McCook, are all that are left of a large famliy. He is an attorney, practicing in the city of New York, and was prominently mentioned for a place in President McKinley's Cabinet. The Regimental Association has made him an honorary member of its organization.

Lieut. Col. D. D. T. Cowen, a son of Judge B. S. Cowen, of Belmont county, Ohio, was thirty-six when commissioned. He was admitted to the bar the day he was twenty-one, and was a leader in his profession. He commanded the regiment on the Kentucky campaign. Your historian was, perhaps, as well acquainted with Col. Cowen as any man in the regiment. He was intellectual, fatherly, courteous, quiet and uncommunicative. The men of the regiment did not know him. His dear wife was dying with consumption, with five small boys and a girl, all helpless. She wrote, pleadingly, for him to come home. As I entered his tent at Nashville,

I found him weeping. He handed me a letter. I said to him, "Colonel, no man in the regiment will blame you." He resigned Feb. 18th, 1863. Eight days after he arrived at his home he buried the mother. He lived an honored citizen of St. Clairsville, and joined his loved one in April, 1889.

Lieut. Col. Charles W. Clancy was promoted from Captain of Company B, Feb. 18, 1863, and to Brevet Colonel May 31, 1865. No man in the regiment had a better record. A physician by profession, a soldier in spirit and bearing. Of his soldier life I cannot dwell. You all know how he received his promotion at Nashville. How sad when the enemy dragged him from his position at Peach Tree, fighting with his face to the front against great odds. How the welkin went up when he returned at Atlanta and led us down to the sea. In every battle his sword flashed to revenge the slaughter of his countrymen. He came home, entered upon his profession, served with honor as representative in the legislature, and died in Smithfield, O , at the age of 58 years.

Major Israel D. Clark was promoted from Capt. of Co. A, and resigned March 8th, 1863, and died in Van Wert, Ohio, in 1883.

Major J. Taylor Holmes was promoted to Major from Captain of Co. G, March 8th, 1863, and was promoted to Lieutenant Colonel, Jan. 31, 1865, but not mustered. Was mustered out with the regiment as Brevet Lieutenant Colonel. Major Holmes was a born gentleman, scholar and soldier. He was publicly and officially complimented for his bravery and efficiency in drill and tactics and was perhaps as well known as any other officer of equal rank in the 14th Corps, for his equestrian appearance on the march, or on the field of battle. Major Holmes, as we still call him, was captured at Lexington, Ky., while sick, and was a prisoner for three months. He was wounded while leading the

Regiment at Jonesboro. He was mustered out with the regiment, entered the law practice, and lives in the city of Columbus, O. By frugality and hard work, he is able to welcome a beautiful old age, which is slowly coming on. He is a loyal Christian soldier and frequently fills the pulpit of the Broad Street M. E. Church, of which he is an honored member. Comrades desiring to find him can call on, or address him, in the National Bank Building, South High street, Columbus, O.

Surgeon Morse resigned May 9th, 1863, and his subsequent history is unknown,

Assistant Surgeon H. M. Duff was from Galion, O. He was frail in body, but an excellent surgeon. He resigned at Atlanta, and died at Galion, O., in 1876.

Surgeon N. S. Hill was promoted from Assistant Surgeon of the 121st Ohio to Surgeon of the 52nd, October 28th, 1864, and died at Neville, O., April 13th, 1896. The regiment was very indignant at his promotion and acceptance over Assistant Surgeon S. A. Simpson. We know nothing of Surgeon Hill's life and death, only that he died and his body was cremated at Cincinnati, O.

Assistant Surgeon S. A. Simpson came to us May 10th, 1864. He won the respect and confidence of the regiment and was mustered out with us and died shortly after the war closed.

Adjutant Charles H. Blackburn resigned November 26th, 1862. His record was excellent, while in the service. He is a prominent attorney in Cincinnatti, O. He has been a partner of General Green B. Raum and has the record of being the best criminal lawyer in Ohio.

Adjutant George A. Masury was appointed from First Lieutenant of Co. I, December 25th, 1862. He was a young man of military bearing, an expert in company and squad drill. He was frail in body and consequently was not credited with a brave heart in the hour of battle. He died shortly after the war, and is buried in Painesville, O.

Quartermaster Israel Fisher resigned November 20th, 1862, and we have no record, since the war.

Quartermaster J. J. Troxell resigned in 1864.

Quartermaster Isaac Stokes was promoted from the ranks to Commissary Sergeant, and to Quartermaster, November 18, 1864 and mustered out with the regiment. Captain Stokes is perhaps the most remarkable man in the regiment. He inlisted in the 70th Ohio, Co. I, and when his son John S. Stokes enlisted in Co H, 52nd Ohio, the father was transferred to our regiment. He gave his age as 36. His son was 30. Both were mustered out with the regiment. The son died many years ago. The Captain lives at 1130 Vine street, Cincinnati, O., at the age of 93. He was 55 when he enlisted. He is somewhat of a poet, having composed many of the songs sung by old Tommy Paine of the same company. Captain Stokes attended the National Encampment at Philadelphia in 1899 and can relate the incidents and experiences with the accuracy of a veteran of fifty.

Chaplain A. L. Petty served with the regiment five months. Jealousy on the part of one of the line officers of the regiment, who prejudiced the officers and men against him, made it hard for the Chaplain in the start, but we believe he has the confidence and esteem of the survivors of the regiment, as a man and minister. He has filled the best appointments in his conference since his return, and retires from active service in the ministry, to his country home near Duncan's Falls, O., beloved and respected by all who knew him.

Chaplain J. S. Keagle came to the regiment at Lee and Gordon's Mills, and left us when Atlanta was taken. He died at Columbus, O., in 1894 at the age of sixty-two. He withdrew from the ministry on his return home and spent part of his subsequent life in the Dayton Soldiers' Home.

Sergeant Major William Freeman was an Englishman. He was wounded at Kenesaw Mountain, by a pick handle being thrown over by the enemy, from which injury he was discharged and died in 1865 in Cleveland, O.

W. D. Scott, Quartermaster Sergeant, was mustered out with the regiment and lives an honored citizen of Denver, Colorado.

James Knisely, Drum Major, has an excellent record. He is living in New Philadelphia, O., always attends the reunions of the regiment and brings with him the tenor drum he carried three years in the service. He is proud of the two bullet holes the enemy put through the drum. He was a member of the regimental band.

THOSE WHO GAVE THEIR LIVES.
COMPANY A.

Killed or died of wounds: Andrus Bowers, Jacob Elder, J. W. Rutan, at Atlanta; J. W. Harper, Jesse Roberts, at Peach Tree.

Died of disease in the hospital at Nashville: Anthony M. Bowers, John Bush, George W. Beck, Matthias Denman, Lester B Foust, James J. Jackson, Isaac N. Johnson and Solomon Hunsacker; at Bowling Green, Ky., Daniel Shrum.

COMPANY B.

Killed in action or died of wounds: John T. Fowler, William F. Carson, Kenesaw; L. D. Mercer, Henry Bargar, James C. Haynes, Peach Tree; Robert N. Mercer, Jonesboro; William M. Fleming, Averysboro. Alfred Downard, captured at Chickamauga, died in Andersonville.

Died in the hospital at Nashville: James Shane, Benjamin F. Brown, Matthias F. Blackburn, Elijah M. Caldwell, George W. Chambers, David Daily, David B. Durbin, Thomas Hunter, Charles S. Miller, James R. Nation, Edwin R. Worthington.

Died at Bowling Green: Samuel Mustard, William Haynes, and John W. Worthington; at Savannah, Georgia: Henry B. Anderson; at Gallatin, Tennessee, Joseph Blazier.

COMPANY C.

Killed in action or died of wounds, William J. Bradfield, James Evans, Linley H. Street, at Kenesaw; Fenton C. Carter, W. F. Beatty, at Peach Tree; Alfred Brister, at Jonesboro; James Chance, at Goldsboro; Boyd Forbes, William F. Lewis, at Resacca.

Died in the hospital at Nashville, Geo. W. Campbell, Mordeica Carter, John Forbes, Asbury Malone, John Malone and Isaac Stidd. Died at Bentonville, John W. Barnes and Emmer B. Clifford, at Harrodsburgh, Ky.; George Golding and Havener Chapman, at Bowling Green, Ky.; and Alexander Hinton at Atlanta.

COMPANY D.

Killed in action or died of wounds, Capt. S. M. Neighbor, Joseph Shacklee, Wm. K. Armstrong, Thomas J. Berkshire, James Beard, James Boyd, John Daugherty, Francis Grace, John Reardon, and Jonathan Sills at Kenesaw; Capt. James M. Summers at Avereysboro; Robert Ferron at Bentonville. Harvey Banks died in Prison Hospital. Obediah Conwell, Levi Conwell, Elisha Wright, at LaVergne; John Lowmiller, at Dallas; Thomas McKee at Resacca; Otto Norris, at Sandersville, Ga.

Died in the hospital at Nashville, Charles Bender, Thomas Chambers, Tillman Clark, Silas Clark, Joseph S.

Evans, Jacob Lambertz, Robert Wineman, Luther Weaver. Died at Murfreesboro, Andrew J. Minnis; at Danville, Ky., John Milligan; at McAfee Church, Albert Sheets.

COMPANY E.

Killed in action or died of wounds: Lieut. James H. Donaldson, Elias Dimmit, Eli. W. Gordon, Samuel M. Hamlon, David Henry, James C. Lease at Peach Tree; John Allman, at Lexington, Ky.; Robert M. Blackburn, at Averysboro; Joseph Hanlon, Isaac N. Winters, at Kenesaw; Otho Linton, at Atlanta; John F. Rightly, at Goldsboro and James W. Sheets, at Jonesboro.

Died in the Hospital at Nashville: Nelson Allen, David H. Allen, John Crawford, Robert B. Connell, Wm. Gillespie, David T. McMasters, Oliver P. Toot, and James Underwood; Edward H. Arthurs, Chattanooga; and James Cunningham, Danville, Ky.

COMPANY F.

Killed in action or died of wounds: Ebenezer Gillespie, Albert E. Crist, Augustus T. Dorsey, Robert J. Stewart at Kenesaw; Thomas Flint, on the Sultana. Uriah Martin, at Goldsboro.

Died in the hospital at Nashville: Joshua Campbell, John Hess, John Kinney, James Lucas, Thomas Nuss, Joseph P. Rader, Jacob Shepherd, John Siler, Asa Vandyne, James E King, Danville, Ky.; Conrad Shipman, Evansville, Indiana; Cornelius Kess, at Pruett's Knob and John W. Sidles, Bowling Green, Ky.

COMPANY G.

Killed in action or died of wounds: Lieut. David F. Miser, Isaac N. Wycoff, at Kenesaw; Jonathan Carman, Benjamin F. Miser, James W. Donaldson, Francis H. Scott,

Peach Tree.   John B. McCarroll, at Jonesboro; and William K. Schultz, at Goldsboro, N. C.

Died in the hospital at Nashville: Thomas G. Grable, John Hales, Robert S. Maxwell, James Peggs, Arthur W. Robb, Stanley Shane, Geo. W. Wallace; at Bowling Green, Ky., Henry K. Crabs, Jacob Angle, Hiram Angle, John Andrews and Jacob Long; at Richmond, Ky., Geo. W. Bain; at Harrodsburgh, Ky., Michael Burchfield; at Gallatin, Tenn., George Barcus; at Lebanon, Ky., Jacob Birch; at Edgefield, Tenn., Lewis Browning; at Columbus, O., Wm. Donaldson; at Louisville, Kentucky, Abram Fickes; at Home, Robert McClave; at Louisville Ky., Wm. J. West.

COMPANY H.

Killed in action or died of wounds: Edgar Flynn, William J. Armstrong, George Courtman, at Atlanta; Ernest Brady, Joseph Bowlby, John J. Farrell, at Kenesaw; William J. Campbell, John Klank, Charles Lespie, Charles W. Smelzer, at Peach Tree; James K. Sowers, at Dallas.

Died in the hospital at Nashville: David S. Dennis, Alvin Goodwin, Thomas Mayhew, Christian Rusy, Enos Reisch; at Bowling Green, Ky., Abram Lewellyn, Jesse Miller, John H. Melvin; at Louisville, Ky., Oliver Rice.

COMPANY I.

Killed: Capt. P. I. Schneider, at Peach Tree; Henry Lotz, Ira H. Pool, Joseph M. Garrison, Thomas Olds, Howard F. Thompson, Henry Webber, at Kenesaw; Michael Habermehl, at Atlanta; John Kraus, at Jonesboro; James Moneysmith, at Perrysville; John M. Pearce, John Robinson, at Buzzard's Roost; Peter Risser, at Bentonville; Aaron I. Brown in prison.

Died in the hospital at Nashville: W. W. Titus, Alexander P. Harkins, Lafayette Lemunyan, Geo. B. Titus; at

Bowling Green, Zopher Randall, Albert Bentley; at Gallatin, Tenn., Lutner Call; at Chattanooga, Tenn., Philo Ray.

COMPANY K.

Killed in action or died of wounds: John Bitner, Thomas Duke, Horace B. Jewell, Elijah McNeal, Samuel Smith, at Peach Tree; Julius Byers, at Buzzard's Roost; Charles Haines, David Kavanaugh, William Mevin, Lemuel Olds, at Kenesaw; and Arthur D. Palmer died in prison. Died in hospital at Nashville: J. H. Genson, Aaron Osmer, William Thompson. At Louisville: Cyrus Baxter, John Burdell and John StClair. At Bowling Green: Oscar L. Perrin and Isaac West. At Gallatin, Tenn., Grant C. Cook.

DISCHARGED FROM HOSPITALS.

Company A.—John Eckfield, Jacob H. Beck, James Carnahan, Samuel Caplinger, Henry Binkhoff, John H. Franklinberg, Benj. M. Golliver, Alexander Kissenger, Levi A. Meely, Sam'l J. Marsh and William H. Payne.

Campany B.—James O. Bates, Walter A. McCullough, George W. Carter, Alex. Alloway, William Barkhurst, James Bond, Thomas Coleman, Thomas Cox, Alexander Davidson, Joseph Devinney, Virginius Daval, William Harrison, J. C. Harrison, Thomas R. Jobes, William H. Lee, George Malone, M. H. McMasters, Joseph Ross, Alfred H. Robinson, Wm. H. Timmerman, Thomas Taylor and John Wagner.

Company C.—James H. Carter, Frank M. Acton, Exum Bailey, Wm. A. Brister, Amos H. Hampton, Joseph W. Hunt, William McDonald, Josiah B. McKee, John H. McEndre, Benj. F. Purkey, Asa T. Patterson, Ellis C. Tomlinson.

Company D.—Wm. S. Dent, Luther B. Ricketts, Alfred Peck, William McFadden, Wm. T. Brown, Resin E.

Bovard, John L. Gordon, David A. Kernes, John L. Kennedy, Peter Lambertz, Abner Loomis, A. W. Lemasters, Wm. Lemasters, James D. Moore, James Potter, Charles M. Rittenhouse, Henry Schweitzer, Wm. E. Tyler, Oliver A. Voeguitz.

Company E —Mordeica McDowell, William S. Wilkin, Mark Albaugh, Moses Boyd, Lewis N. Carman, Thomas Crown, Geo. W. Dally, Ellis Dalrymple, Alexander Douglass, Rezin P. Mansfield, W. J. McCann, Thomas McKee, D. T. McMasters, Robert Nelson, Calvin Newburn, Dan'l Prosser, William Ryan, William Rhine, Thomas C. Scott, Lycurgus Shearer, Isaac Toot, Richard Thompson, George Wilson.

Company F.—Samuel M. Gordon, Benj. F. Thomas, James McAvoy, Michael Allen, Wm. Bennett, Robt. Carpenter, Frank F. Cook, Dorsey Danford, Alfred Doty, Daniel Groves, William Gatton, Edward Huffman, Henry Huffman, John Jobes, Joseph H. Jones, Alex. Landers, G. W. Lindsay, W. T. Minamyer, Christian May, Singleton Owens, John Rush, Joshua Richardson, John Shipman, Hezekiah Saffle, John R. Trigg.

Company G.—John R. Berry, Wm. McCook, Samuel H. Wyant, A. M. Stevenson, Samuel Arnold, John Berry, Hamilton Barcus, P. Y. Barnes, Samuel Blackburn, Jonathan A. Cole, Clinton Critzer, L. B. Douglass, Emery P. Douglass, Robert S. Dunbar, John R. Dungan, John E. Goodwin, Tinlis Hawser, Richard W. Jobe, Cyrus H. Jenkins, William Kelly, Ezra D. Lawrence, John Polen, Benjamin C. Rex, Thos. G. Stevenson, James Wallace, Julius B. Work, John S. Wright.

Company H.—Daniel Byrnes, Edward Conley, William Cox, Joseph W. Norton, Thomas Payne, Adam Story, Elias Stoneburner, Albert Sewell.

Company I.—William E. Clayton, Peter H. Clinton, Griffeth Hunter, William Bachier, Laramore J. Baxter, Albert Button, Daniel S. Charlton, Martin Emhoff, George B. Harris, J. W. Householder, A. P. Lawrence, William Myers, Thomas S. McGarrah, Frank Robinson, Frederick Seivert.

Company K.—James O. Bamber, Vincent Hawkins, Francis M. James, Thomas McNeal, James McNeal, Barney McDarrah, Timothy McDowell, George W. Matthews, James F. Merrion, Paul W. Woodward.

DISCHARGED FROM HOSPITALS OR AT EXPIRATION OF SERVICE, WHO SERVED THREE YEARS.

Company A.—Sergeant James H. Scott, wounded both thighs, severe; Corporal Robert E. Baxter, prisoner; John Graham; Samuel B. Marshall, Hospital steward; Thomas, Merrit, McCaslin, McGonagle.

Company B.—Lewis D. Mercer, prisoner; Oliver M. Shane, Henry H. Flemming, Joseph Brown, David Paxton, Isaac Howard and David Paxon, prisoners.

Company C.—William Carter, James W. Folger, Webster Folger, William G. Hilton, James W. Lynne, wounded, John W. Merrill and Jerome Miller.

Company D.—John W. Baltzly, Andersonville; Levi Shull, Josiah Brolyer, John Brown, John Davy, Henry Foreman, C. H. Fishley, Isaac Howard, prisoners; Anthony Hartley, prisoner; David McFee, wounded.

Company E.—J. B. Mansfield, wounded; W. B. Crown, wounded; Joseph M. Thompson, wounded twice; David U. McCullough, wounded; John C. Brown, leg amputated; B. M. Culbertson, wounded; Salathia Catterell, David Dimmitt,

ROBERT GATES, CO. F.

Alexander Gracy, arm amputated; David L. Miller, W. H. Reynolds, wounded; James Sullivan, George Thomas, wounded; Silas Yocum, wounded; William W. Ault, prisoner.

Company F.—Anthony T. Lockwood, Isaac Gates, wounded; Alexander C. Crist, wounded; F. C. Kirkland, Conrad M. McCabe.

Company G.—Albert E. McCue, Emory P. Smith, prisoner; Isaac Baughart, arm amputated; Mord M. Cook, Robert McIntosh, wounded; T. H. Montgomery, arm amputated; Frank McElravy.

Company H.—John Miller, Henry H. Pickell, John Cummins, Lorenza Azbill, John Dewise, Richard Foneroe, Samuel Hardy, wounded; George B. Hodgson, wounded; Patrick Hamilton, prisoner, escaped from Florence, South Carolina; Jacob Mentz, Bartlet Montgomery, Barney Mucker, Charles Pierce, John W. Steed, William Struby, Jacob Warner.

Company I.—Theodore Bartell, prisoner; Richard Blodgett, wounded; N. H. Bostwick, wounded twice in the same battle and taken prisoner; Frank Brunhofer, Deming B. Fish, prisoners; Phillip Shaffer, wounded through the chest.

Company K.—Samuel J. Hoskins, prisoner; Leander C. Kelley, W. B. Beatty, W. W. Chulip, prisoners; Horace B. Church, William W. Driskell, prisoner; Josiah Dye, Alonzo Fuller, prisoners; Michael Hearn, William Potts, Frederick Rathgiver, Hiram Rice, Byron Smith, prisoners; Levi Walters, wounded.

TRANSFERRED TO THE VETERAN RESERVE CORPS AND TO THE 69TH OHIO.

Company A.—Isaac N. Groscost, John Baker, Daniel Reiley, Henry Bieran, John H. Howard, Alfred Kniss, Lycurgus Moffett, John L. Rhoden, William R. Tutor.

Company B.—John Barkeimer, recruit; Charles A. Brooks, recruit; John Harrison, recruit; J. A. Householder, W. M. Johnson, Harry Kauffman recruit; Reese O. King, recruit; John P. Kendrick, Elba C. Morgan, John J. Nation, Thomas E. Paxon, recruit; Scott Roe, John Seals, Joel H. Smith, recruit; Robert E. Wilson, recruit; George A. Walker, recruit.

Company C.—Charles H. Bowers, James P. Carter, Henry Crawford, Cement Hicks, William L. Patton, Isaac Teats recruit.

Company D.—Sylvester Baker, Lemon Chambers, recruit; James Douglass recruit; Jacob Goerlitz, Samuel T. Hensil, John Kirk, John Keyes, John Kirkpatrick, David Markley, William A Ohaver, Lewis Glass, Gunboat.

Company E.—A. C. Blackburn, George Fenwick, recruit; Vachel Gallaway, Morse I. Gray, James W. Harper, recruit; James L. Rogers, recruit; Thomas D. Shannon, James W. Sanford, Thomas Welch, recruit.

Company F.—Thomas Boyers, James B. Day, recruit; Robert A. Hammond, Jacob W. Moore, Franklin Poulson, recruit; Morgan Vandyne, recruit; George W. Wallace, recruit.

Company G.—Richard B. McFerrin, recruit; Enoch Probert, recruit; Greenbury Phillips, recruit; Abner D. Richards, recruit; Franklin Smith, Edward J. Springer, recruit, Edward Wilson.

Company H.—James Fallis, Charles Brown, Wm. Evan, Benj. L. Harris, John A. Higgins, Charles Lespie, Washington Magee, Isaac McMullen, David Walters, John Wiley, Lewis Woodward, recruits; John W, Doll, veteran reserve corps; Robert Melon, Henry Prinzell, Sebastian Sowers.

Company I.—Lucius Boyden, signal corps, Theodore Schenler.

Company K.—John Murphy, George Ainsworth, Asel Canfield, Lewis Downs, Charles Firman, Joseph Marshall, Samuel Riddle.

NO RECORD FOUND.

Company A.—John Binkley, John Cusick, Patrick Hill, Calvin Hill, Charles W. Huges, Thomas Lilly, Osborn E. Miller, John O'brien, Edwin W. Roice, John White, Martin Zelliner and Joshua Zelliner.

Company C.—Franklin Neff, Elisha B. Watson and Calvin Williams.

Company D.—Alexander Brown, John D. Blouse, Alfred J. Neff and John Spring.

Company E.—Andrew Shannon

Company F —Robert Cunningham and Thomas Nuss.

Company G.—William Gerrin and John Kirkpatrick.

Company H.—George K. Farrington, William Brinning, Joseph Blundell, Daniel Bonners, Charles Cornell, W. H. Dellerty, John Dury, John Elder, John Gable, John Henry, Josiah Lewis, John A. Mayes, Henry Mittendorf, Patrick Murphy, William Riley, Harry Smith, John A Sellins, E. T Snyder, Joseph Skiver, Henry C. Wiley.

Company I.—Ezra Beebe, Philip Boss, Frank Barrett, Adelbert Curtis, Ransel Cutler, Amos Eaton, William Green, Stewart S. Hukill, James Phipps, George Simons, Hiram Stratton.

Company K.—Edward O'Conner, Grant C. Cook, Elisha Dowdney, Henry Eldridge, James Hawkins, John Kunsley, Frank Littlefair, Patrick Lyons, Terrance McNalley, Theodore Miller, John Obrien, Patrich Raney, Jacob H. Scribner, C. H. Wiles, David Wintermoot.

MUSTERED OUT WITH THE REGIMENT.

Campany A.—Captain W. H. Bucke, Sergeant Robert M. Sproul, Corporals James Conaway, George W. Holtry and John S. Baxter, Calvin Billings, William H. Anschultz, James W. Baxter, John K. Baxter, George W. Beamer, Daniel Brittsan, William Baney, John I. Cable, William Calvert, James Cashin, Henry Dryer, Nimrod Emerson, Jeremiah Foulke, Tovanion Goliver, James Highland, Joseph Kannel, Christian Kerns, Frank W. Leslie, John W. Murphy, Benjamin Melchi, Jonathan Myers, Thomas McGill, Samuel Murphy, William O'Neal, James O'Hara, John H. Styner, Christian Trubee, John J. Vangundy, Joshua Walters, Archibald Winget.

Company B.—Lieutenant W. A. Judkins, Sergeants Theodore Humphreyville, Joseph T. Withrow, H. B. Mercer and David M. Runyan; Corporals Morris Graham, James H. McMasters, Leander Jones, Ross Noble, Samuel Grimshaw and Benjamin B. Foster, David R. Brisbin, Pinckney Bone; Musicians Edward Brown, Elza V. Cox, James Davidson, John T. Dugan, Columbus Evans, Gilbert S. Fleming, William Giles, Isaac R. Henry, John W. Hastings, John W. Hicks, Oliver Hicks, George F. Irwin, William Kirk, Wm. Kirk, Jr., Benjamin H. Kirk, Jacob Myers, James McDonald, Oliver McGrew, Allen T. McMasters, John W. McGlaughlin, Campbell Miller, George W. Pierce, William Roe, George W. Tweedy, Uriah H. Updegraff and George W. Wilson.

Company C.—Captain Abisha C. Thomas, Lieutenant Christopher W. Grimes, First Sergeant William Starbuck, Sergeant Edwin D. Patterson, Corporals Newell H. Buchanan, William C. Deems, Joseph A. Parsons, Charles T. Whittacre, Charles W. Tillet, Harrison Moore and John W. Hance, Benjamin Ammon, Thomas B. Barnes, John Bailey, Isaac

B. Clift, William Colvin, Wm. H. Coventry, George W. Colvig, John Dilliha, George W. Day, Isaac Hayes, Robert W. Harris, James Hines, William Hadley, Robert Humphrey, John N. Hunt, William Latham, Sherrow W. Parker, Wm. H. Piper, Thomas Petticord, John Rucker, John W. Stubbs, James T. Woodland, W. W. Wildman and Robert Warrick.

Company D.—Lieutenant William H. Ray, First Sergeant W. P. Mulvane, Sergeant William L. Laffer and John Smith, Jr; Corporals George W. Exline, Thomas W. Sargeant, Jeremiah B. Souder and Theodore D. Neighbor, Johnson Brown, David Carr, William Chambers, Thomas P. Cordery, Robert Crooks, Elijah Crossland, Eldridge Davis, William Davy, John Davy, Charles Howard, William Heckler, David Hines, Benjamin Howell, Emanuel Keffer, David Lint, Andrew J. Miller, Maynard Mayberry, Thomas Malone, Solomon McPherson, Silas C. Neff, George W. Neighbor, Gilbert L. Patterson, Jehu Peck, James H. Ray, Peter P. Reeves, Francis M. Shaffer, William H. Shull, Lafayette Smith, John S. Stough, Jacob Strickmaker, James Trueman, Valentine Wright.

Company E.—Captain William H. Lane, First Lieutenant A B. McIntire, First Sergeant Daniel T. Hustcroft, Sergeants David King and Nixon B. Stewart, Corporals Elmer Everson, Thomas A. Thompson and Henry H. Scott, Daniel Arnold, Franklin Carnahan, George Davis, Henry H. Day, John Fellows, William J. Funston, James Fenwick, Nelson Householder, John Johnson, Joshua Johnson, John Keiley, Thomas B. Mansfield, Bazil H. Maxwell, Daniel McElfresh, Andrew McManus, James Moore, Bartley Moore, John A. Nelson, Hiram G Price, George W. Quillen, William Stone, John N. South, Andrew Taylor and Benjamin F. Wilson.

JOHN W. DAVY, CO. D.

Company F.—Captain Samuel C. Hutchinson, First Lieutenant Sylvester L. Brice, First Sergeant Thomas B. Cammond, Sergeants James McFadden, Anthony Lockwood, John W. Cess, and William M. Swain Corporals Michael Loy, Elijah R. Hudson, Thomas Tyrell and Peter Griffin, John Anthony, Martin Baker, Eli Barnes, Volney Blue, David Dillon, William Duval, Stewart Doty, Robert Gates, James Gates, John J. Gillespie, Washington Gillespie, Johnson Hammond, James Holland, George W. Johnson, John Moore, William W. Moore, John McVey, John C. Pittman, Martin Purtyman, Salathiel Pugh, Hiram K. Rader, William A. South, Joshua Swaney, James Thornberry, James Tyrell, Isaac Vandyne, Jonathan Vandyne, Perry Wright.

Company G.—First Lieut. Lemuel W. Duff; First Sergeant Abram R. Holmes, Sergeants Joseph C. Rogers, Samuel M. Pyle, Ross E. Rex, Styles W. Porter. Corporal James Taylor and Johnson Davis, Hamilton Wallace, musician; William V. Baim, James C. Bowers, Thomas Burchfield-George Berry, Thomas M. Burns, William P. Barnes, Nathan Gosset, Thomas C. Grader, Brice R. Gruber, James E. Jackman, James M. Kain, John McIntosh, Robert McIntosh, James L. Porter, Charles Roberts, John Rhinehart, Johsua Saltsman, Benjamin E Saltsman, Joseph Swan, William H. Stephenson, David P. Stephenson, James Wallace, Jr., David Walters and Milton B. Wyant.

Company H.—First Lieut. Julius Armstrong, Second Lieut. Gossler Rudolph, First Sergeant Isaac L. Mills, Sergeants Samuel A. Harper, William C. Noone, and John W. Coleman; Corporal John W. Bowen, John Bonhart, James Budd, Osborne Belt, George Cahoo, Benjamin F. Clark, Edward Greiner, Richard Harms, John Harris, George B. Hodgson, John Martin, Joseph H. Miller, William Miller, Aaron

Mills, Robert McMullen, George W. Parker, John S. Stokes, Digory Sholl, Wesley Woodward and John H. Wagoner.

Company I.—Capt., Frank B. James; First Sergeant, David R. Roe; Sergeants Howard B. Treat, John Lanaghan; Corporals, Thomas Hunter, Horace T. Clark, George P. Cogswell, and John Stough. Phineas A. Thompson, William Barclay, William H. Close, Arthur T. Corlett, Matthias Haffele, William Lockard, James McCutcheon, Samuel Miller, John N. Norton, Herman Pilz, James Porter, Robert Robinson, Thomas H. Rhenark, Joseph Summer, John M. Ulsenheimer, Charles Whittern.

Company K.—Capt., Edward L. Anderson; Second Lieut., Samuel J. Brent; First Sergeant, George Wilcox; Sergeant, Henry Brakeman; Corporal George Kueny, and Michael Madden, Lewis Fink, Francis Falter, John L. Gordon, Henry Holden, James Hudson, Simon P. Heller, Andrew J. Jeffers, Henry Koch, James Lineback, John K. McKenzie, Blair H. Puffenbarger, Valentine Strode, William L. Troxel, Andrew Weisfoot.

CAMP OF CO. A — LEE & GORDON'S MILL, GEORGIA, MARCH 1864.

L. M. Strayer Collection

CORP. JOHN W. HANCE, CO. C.

FIRST LIEUT. GEORGE A. MASURY, ADJUTANT

CAPT. SAMUEL C. HUTCHISON, CO. F.

THOMAS H. KIRKLAND, CO. F.

J. B. Work, *Re-Union of Col. Dan McCook's Brigade*

CAPT. SAMUEL ROTHACKER, CO. G.

SERGT. STYLES W. PORTER, CO. G.

PHILANDER Y. BARNES, CO. G.

GROUP OF 52nd OHIO OFFICERS AT LEE & GORDON'S MILL, MARCH 1864. FROM LEFT: LIEUT. DAVID F. MISER, CO. G; LIEUT. FRANK B. JAMES, CO. K, LIEUT. JULIUS ARMSTRONG, CO. F; LIEUT. JAMES H. DONALDSON, CO. E; LT. COL. CHARLES W. CLANCY; MAJOR J. TAYLOR HOLMES. TWO BLACK SERVANTS STAND AT FAR RIGHT.

INDEX

Pages on which photographs or illustrations appear are boldfaced.

197, **234**
Doty, Stewart, 203
Duff, Francis W., 55
Duff, Henry M., 12, 55, 136, 139, 208
Duff, Lemuel W., 199
Dunbar (steamboat), 71
Duncan Falls, Ohio, 209
Dunham, Lucius T., 189
Durham's Station, N.C., 169
Dustin's Brigade, 161

Eatonton, Ga., 146
Ebenezer Church, 148
Edgefield, Tenn., 34
Edisto River, 155
Elmwood, Ill., 200
Elson, Parker A., 11, **46,** 196
Ely's Ford, 173
Enfield rifles, 164
Erie County, Ohio, 202
Ewell, Richard S., 173

Fahnestock, Allen L., 115
Fair Oaks, battle of, 151
Fairfield County, Ohio, 200
Fallis Creek, 157
Farrow, Robert, 163
Fayetteville, N.C., 157, 158
Fearing, Benjamin D., 152, 161, 163
Fearing's Brigade, 160
Fellows, Charles, 119
Fenn's Bridge, 147, 194
Fifteenth Corps, 158, 177
Fifty-second Ohio Association, 187-188, 206
Fisler, Israel, 12, 209
Fleming, William M., 159
Flinn, Edgar, 133
Florence, Ala., 139
Flushing, Ohio, 199
Forrest, Nathan Bedford, 44, 139
Fort Delaware, 123
Fort Donelson, battle of, 75
Fort Fisher, 167, 179
Fort McAllister, 149
Fort Negley, 38
Fort Sumter, 158
Fort Wood, 74
Fourteenth Corps, 67, 94, 95, 98, 106, 152, 156, 158, 162, 171, 176, 177, 178, 180, 207
Fourth Corps, 67, 103, 140
Fowler, John T., 117
Frankfort, Ky., 18
Franklin County, Ohio, 149
Franklin Pike, 38, 47, 52

Franklin, Tenn., 52, 53, 127
Fredericksburg, Va., 173
Freeman, William, 88, 126, 210
Fry, Speed S., 20, 22
Fulton County, Ga., 138
Funston, William J., **33,** 43

Galion, Ohio, 208
Galt House, 20, 21
Ganley's Mills, 77
Garrard, Kenner, 105
Gates, Robert, **217**
Gaylesville, Ala., 140
Geauga County, Ohio, 121
Georgia Railroad, 144
Georgia Troops,
  Infantry:
  8th Georgia, 90
  23rd Georgia, 164
Gettysburg, battle of, 49
Giffen, Peter, **72,** 199
Gilbert, Charles C., 22, 23, 25, 28, 29
Gillem, Alvan C., 138
Goldsboro, N.C., 149, 151, 159, 165, 167, 170
Gooding, Michael, 95
Gordon, Eli, 130, 133
Gordon, John B., 62
Gossett, Nathan, 200
Grace, Francis, 120, 194
Granger, Gordon, 55, 60, 67
Grant, Ulysses S., 49, 68, 70, 73, 74, 95, 96, 114, 151, 167, 168, 170, 173, 176, 206
Granville, Ohio, 202
Gray's Station, 77
Great Pee Dee River, 156
Grimes, Christopher W., 140, **185,** 191
Grimshaw, Samuel, 190
Gurley, Frank, 54

Halleck, Henry W., 170, 172
Hampton County, S.C., 154
Hampton, Wade, 154, 155, 157
Hance, John W., **227**
Hancock, Winfield S., 178
Hanging Rock, S.C., 156
Hanlin, Joseph, 120
Hanlin, Samuel M., 130, 131, 133
Hanlon, E. Tappan, 135, 197
Hardee, Colonel, 164
Hardee, William J., 149, 158, 160, 161
Hardee's Corps, 29, 117
Hardy, Samuel, 202-203
Harker's Brigade, 99
Harmon, Oscar F., 84, 94, 115, 119